"What a great gift Bill has given to us in this book! Pick it up. Read it slowly. What could be more important than to mine the depths of the grace of God—especially in a world where we continually fall back into a desperate and hopeless attempt to do what Christ has already done? Bill not only does a masterful job of mining these depths, but he also doesn't shy away from the myriad of 'Yeah, but' questions we all ask when faced with the radical reality of what Christ has done for us: a new life, no condemnation, adoption as a child of the King. Wow! What can we add? Nothing. Cease striving. Lay it down. Great book!"

DEL TACKETT
Architect and host of *The Truth Project*

"Bill Tell has written a tremendously encouraging book for anyone caught in the bindings of performance-based religion. His insights may challenge long-held assumptions about what God wants from you and will lead you to a life of deep joy."

AMY SIMPSON
Author, *Anxious: Choosing Faith in a World of Worry*

"When we meet Jesus, up close and personal, we accept the unconditional grace of being accepted into God's family. But for many of us, after that, we go to work trying to please God by what we do. Unfortunately, we are wired by our Christian culture to try to work our way into God's presence as believers. Travel with Bill Tell as he unlocks the secret of living a close, vibrant relationship with our closest friend, Jesus. This is a life-changing message that you'll want to share with your small group or Bible study. As people grasp the truth of God's unconditional acceptance of them in Jesus, you'll see them change the same way I saw Jesus transforming Bill's life."

LAUREN LIBBY
International president/CEO, TWR International

"The question 'What does God think of me?' can frighten us and even make us feel enslaved and defeated. *Lay It Down* not only engenders freedom and rest from our performing; it encourages obedience and holiness based on what God thinks of us. Pick up *Lay It Down*, and find rest for your weary, busy soul."

ROD MAYS
Executive pastor, Mitchell Road Presbyterian Church, Greenville, South Carolina

"In this refreshing book, Bill Tell identifies the lies that many in the church believe, lies that keep them in bondage, lies that keep them in sin, and lies that keep them from enjoying God's extravagant love. Not only does he expose the lies, Bill points us to the truth. Through his extensive knowledge of Scripture as well as his own experience, Bill shows us the way to true freedom and joyful obedience."

MARK BATES
Senior pastor, Village Seven Presbyterian Church, Colorado Springs, Colorado

"Writing from his own experience and his thorough knowledge of Scripture, Bill Tell shows us how to move from performance-based living into the glorious freedom the gospel is meant to bring. This book will benefit all believers regardless of their stage of maturity in the Christian life."

JERRY BRIDGES
Author, *The Pursuit of Holiness*

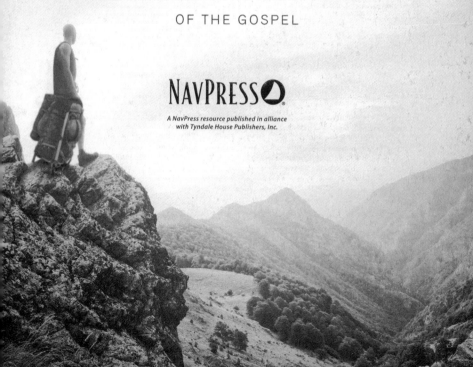

BILL TELL

lay it down

LIVING IN THE FREEDOM
OF THE GOSPEL

NavPress

*A NavPress resource published in alliance
with Tyndale House Publishers, Inc.*

NavPress is the publishing ministry of The Navigators, an international Christian organization and leader in personal spiritual development. NavPress is committed to helping people grow spiritually and enjoy lives of meaning and hope through personal and group resources that are biblically rooted, culturally relevant, and highly practical.

For more information, visit www.NavPress.com.

The Team:
Don Pape, Publisher
David Zimmerman, Acquisitions Editor

Cover design by Ron Kaufmann
Cover photograph of cloudscape copyright © Blue Wren/DollarPhotoClub. All rights reserved.
Cover photograph of mountain and hiker copyright © petarpaunchev/DollarPhotoClub. All rights reserved.
Cover photograph of backpack copyright © Alex Ishchenko/DollarPhotoClub. All rights reserved.

Library of Congress Cataloging-in-Publication Data

Tell, Bill.
  Lay it down : living in the freedom of the gospel / by Bill Tell.
    pages cm
  Includes bibliographical references.
  ISBN 978-1-61291-820-4
  1. Liberty—Religious aspects—Christianity. 2. Salvation—Christianity. I. Title.
  BT810.3.T45 2015
  248.4—dc23   2014048054

Contents

Foreword

As our team travels various continents, we are repeatedly riveted by two realities. Everyone on this earth carries an enormous thirst for lasting, personal freedom. And most simply don't know where to look for the water.

In *Lay It Down*, you have come to the headwaters of freedom. Not the freedom of religious condolence or psychological coping. Not even the self-awarded liberty promised by many in the church, but the freedom of the original gospel. It is the freedom Jesus promised for your personal journey, your family, your community, and your friendships *today*.

While "original," these truths of grace offering such freedom are not at all "common." They have been buried under the rubble of much misunderstanding, misrepresentation, and confusion. So you may be astonished to learn in *Lay It Down* that you are exceedingly freer than you ever imagined. Such is the gospel of Jesus, who promised that after tasting these waters, you would never again seek another freedom.

Bill Tell insightfully explains that freedom also escapes many of us because we're so familiar and comfortable with captivity. Many of us "lifers" are not even looking for a way out of "serving time." Through decades of learning to perform to earn our freedom, many of us have concluded that this dutiful but largely lifeless existence is all there is. That our disillusionment and bondage are normal. Numb and listless, we've stopped hoping for a different way, content with a stagnant parody of freedom. We've forgotten to seek fresh water any longer.

You'll see through the windows of Bill's story that, while coming to Jesus brings us eternal life, it doesn't automatically unearth the unresolved issues of our lives. We may have considered the hope of becoming free *from* our unresolved life issues but counted the process too costly to pursue freedom *to* a life of joy and influence. We disastrously undervalue freedom. Attempting to avoid our reality, we convince ourselves we can manage or bury our stuff, tragically ignoring the fact that all unresolved life issues are buried alive. It doesn't matter whether they come from our families of origin, our own poor choices, or the violations that others inflicted upon us. Our unresolved life issues remain buried alive—and become a lot of work for others.

His first institutional training being in chemistry, Bill Tell brings to his research the thought process of a scientist. Bill is a master at asking the right questions. He is also seasoned in articulating the nuanced differences of true answers from false. Part of the gift of *Lay It Down* is to be guided by someone capable of confronting long-held clichés with the clarity of well-reasoned insight.

Did we mention that Bill is a good friend of ours? We know this story. We even know people who would not talk with him or hang around him before the transformation you will read about in this book. It overwhelms and astounds us to watch the before and after of God's grace at work in Bill. None of this may have taken place without the gift of his wife, Sue Tell. She faithfully endured his bluffing and loved him intently *before* freedom began replacing his unresolved life issues.

Lay It Down is a small book with enormous implications. Everyone in the next restaurant, refugee camp, or ministry you walk into needs this rare message of hope and freedom. But first it must find you. This truth will set you free, but only if you trust it. We urge you to carefully grapple through *Lay It Down*, for if you trust a lie while thinking it is truth, you will long remain in an unwelcome prison.

The author Joseph Cooke titled his autobiographical book *Free for the Taking*, a classic work on grace that was written a generation ago and is reminiscent of *Lay It Down*. It turns out the gospel of God's grace not only leads to freedom but also is free for the taking; through infinite sacrifice, Jesus makes it this way for us. We hope that you cherish this free gift *today* and that tomorrow you will secure *Lay It Down* for more thirsty pilgrims.

Friends, welcome to the fountain of freedom.

Bill Thrall, Bruce McNicol, and John Lynch
coauthors of *The Cure, Bo's Café,* and *Behind The Mask,* and
team members (with Bill Tell) of Truefaced, Inc.,
and Center for the Cure

Acknowledgments

WRITING A BOOK is not an individual effort. It requires the combined energy of a lot of people. And personal growth into whom God has planned us to be never happens in isolation; we need special God-given friends speaking truth into our lives. Without these there would be no book to write.

First I need to acknowledge those who spoke truth into my life and helped me discover the freedom that is mine in the gospel. My friend Bill Thrall is one of the authors of *TrueFaced* and *The Cure*; he has carefully mentored me in the gospel of grace these past fourteen years, and I owe him and the entire TrueFaced team thanks for a transformed life. Milt Bryan guided Sue and me through a life-changing counseling intensive. Alan Andrews, friend and former U.S. President of The Navigators, has faithfully loved, guided, and protected us since our twenties. These and so many others shaped our lives so that a book could be born.

And then there are those who were so key in influencing me to tell my story. First I have to acknowledge Mike Miller, who during his tenure as publisher of NavPress constantly believed in me and encouraged me to write. Without Mike and his terrific friendship I would never have undertaken this project. Don Simpson and David Zimmerman, my NavPress editors, expertly guided me, building on Mike's enthusiasm and keeping me going. David's expertise has been invaluable. And then there are all those who read the manuscript and gave such helpful feedback. Patrick Kochanasz and my Cru friend Steve Kammer were invaluable. Dr. Christopher Morton, a 2011 Tyndale Lecturer at Cambridge, subjected the manuscript to his theological microscope. My son Jeff, pastor of New Life Burbank (PCA), did his best to keep Dad from wandering into serious error. My other son, Dave, inspired me by being the first published author in our family. And then there is my wife, Sue, who not only has been a fellow traveler on this journey, but also relentlessly read and reread the manuscript and gently introduced me to grammar I never knew existed!

And to all who have heard me teach over the years and asked, "Do you have this in writing?"—thank you.

Introduction

THIS IS A book about freedom—about allowing the freedom
Jesus died to give us to transform our lives. Why write about
freedom? Three reasons. First, living in "the glorious freedom
of the children of God" (Romans 8:21, NIV) is at the very
heart of the gospel. Tim Keller writes, "Everything about
the Christian gospel is freedom. Jesus' whole mission was an
operation of liberation."[1] Jesus didn't die His horrific death
and suffer the forever unequaled punishment of God only
to free us from judgment and give us a future in heaven; the
Son of God lived and died so we could begin experiencing
the glories of eternal life *now* and the radical life-changing
freedom of the gospel *today*! It is a freedom that changes
everything about us; it's a change we desperately need.

When we decide to trust the gospel, Brennan Manning
says, we have enrolled in "the school of freedom."[2] To not live
in gospel freedom is sin—serious sin. It is an adamant refusal
to embrace the work God desires to do in our lives, a work

that dearly cost Him. To not live in gospel-given freedom is to *distrust* that God knows what is best for us—and it is our *trust* that pleases Him the most (Hebrews 11:6). For some reason we think that the boundaries we create for ourselves are safer and healthier than the freedoms we are given in the gospel. This is a stinging slap in the face of God. We are declaring we know better than He does. I have a hunch that nothing grieves God more deeply than our distrust of His goodness and love for us, which we discover and experience only as we live in the fullness of our gospel freedom.

Donald Gray, in his book *Jesus, the Way to Freedom*, writes,

> We are freed not only from the fear of death but also
> from the fear of life; we are freed for new life, a life
> that is trusting, hopeful, compassionate. God wants
> us to be well and whole now. That is the good news.[3]

Well and whole . . . *now*! No shame making us hide, no chains binding us to our past, no captivity to unbreakable compulsive sins. This wellness and wholeness is found only in one place—in one relationship: in God's protective love and healing freedom.

Second, as I speak to students and young people around the country, I find that the New Testament is not seen as very good news. The standards for living a godly life are high, and fulfilling them (and thus becoming acceptable to God) seems impossible. One young person put it this way: "Why come to a book every day that makes you feel like a failure?"

Too many people read the Bible and miss the good news of freedom.

Third, this is a book about freedom because it is a book about me. What you are about to read is highly autobiographical. You will see a successful leader with a dark side. You will see the lies that held me captive and the things I craftily hid for years. As you read, please handle me carefully.

These are things I can now share because I realize they don't define who I am. I was free and didn't know it. In the midst of a "dark night of the soul," glimpses of gospel freedom pierced my darkness and I began to grasp—hesitantly at first—the freedom Jesus so intensely wanted me to have.

Do I still hear the chains of captivity rattling in the background? You bet. Probably every day. But they are the rattling lies of our enemy. They no longer need to control my motives, my decision making, my actions. They no longer tell me who I am. There is now a voice speaking to me that tells me truth—truth that releases me to live as God intended. Free.

You have your own lies that hold you captive. As I share my lies, reflect on yours. Then as I share how the gospel sets me free, allow the gospel to set you free. I'm trusting that when you close the last chapter, this book will no longer be about how the gospel set *me* free, but how the gospel sets *you* free.

I need to tell you two things this book is not.

First, this is not a book about independence. "Christianity promises to make man free," Anglican priest William R. Inge writes; "it never promises to make them independent."[4] Freedom and independence are polar opposites. The former leads to wellness and wholeness. The latter leads only to disillusionment and emptiness. Freedom always moves us toward people and into community (Galatians 5:13), and so freedom allows us to love and be loved. Independence separates and isolates, leading to deep loneliness. Independence says, "I do not need you. I am self-sufficient." On the other hand, freedom protects me with a healthy dependence; it lets others love me by meeting my needs. God has created us with needs so we can be loved. Freedom positions me where others can speak truth to me; in independence I am alone and therefore deceived.

In Jesus' parable of the prodigal son we find a young man who confused the freedom he had in the love of his father with the deceptive allure of independence. That young man discovered that independence does not work. Not even a little. Ever. Returning home and being a slave would be better than the deceitful bill of goods labeled independence.

Second, this is not a comprehensive theology on the gospel. We will travel through large parts of the gospel landscape that we often miss to our deepest detriment. We are going to focus on how the gospel frees *us*. But the gospel is not just about us—it is about the glory of the triune God. The New Testament repeatedly tells us we believe and suffer for the sake of *His* name.

As you read, you will be following the trail of my footprints as I discovered in the gospel the freedom that was already mine in this life. There are a lot of gospel places my feet still need to tread. Hopefully you have been places I have yet to go, and you can add chapters to this book.

As you journey with me, may the shackles that bind you loosen and drop off. May the chains that have held you captive become only distant rattles. But as you read, handle yourself carefully. Don't let the chains of the past become sources of shame and condemnation.

CHAPTER I

Into Dark Depths

THERE WAS NO air in the basement guest room. My heart was pounding. I was dripping with sweat. The room was spinning at warp speed, and I was clutching the bed lest I be flung helplessly across the room.

I managed to get my feet on the floor and sit on the edge of the bed. Whatever was happening, it seemed like I would have more control sitting up than lying down. Control was important. It was still dark. I turned on the light . . . four in the morning.

My wife and I were a thousand miles from home. We had left the day before to participate in a missions conference in Illinois, at one of our former churches. The days were crammed full—four days of conference activities and every meal scheduled with close friends and financial supporters. We were eagerly looking forward to reconnecting with many of the special people in our lives. And yet here I was, scared like I had never been in my life.

Elbows on my knees, head in my hands, I sat fighting for control. Tears were rolling down my checks. Then it happened: Overwhelming feelings of dread I never knew existed washed over me in debilitating waves, each one filling me with greater fear and confusion.

In a few hours the Sunday morning I had been anticipating would dawn—a day filled with magnificent worship and overflowing with dear friends. It was supposed to be a good day. Now all that was to be good in the coming day morphed into fear-filled encounters. The thought of being with people was more than I could handle. I couldn't do it.

By this time Sue was awake and aware that something was wrong. The only thing I could say was, "I can't. I can't do it." This became my recurring reply for the next ten months.

Sue went to church by herself that morning and canceled all our appointments for the day. I stayed behind to rebuild my reserves so I could go to the evening service. People were expecting my presence there; I was a long-time missionary of the church, a vice president of The Navigators with responsibility for our student ministries across the country. I needed to show up. A day by myself should replenish whatever it was that had drained out of me.

Yet as we left for the evening service, I was filled with anxiety and a sense that being in a friend-filled public was beyond my ability. Yet it seemed reasonable I could dredge up enough adrenaline and willpower to do it. There had always been reserves to draw on. And after all, I was a leader and *ought* to be there. And so we went.

For a small wall of protection, I sat with Sue in the very last row in one of my favorite sanctuaries—one filled with wonderful memories. But tonight, the organ I loved to listen to was harsh and way too loud. The congregational singing sounded like the raucous crowd at a hockey game. It was awful. The conference speaker seemed to be constantly yelling at me in the back row. After the service, friends surrounded us, and with each handshake and hug I felt something draining out of me. I returned to our hosts' home worse than when I had left, emptier than had I ever felt in my life. My reserves that had always been there were gone. At least tonight I had lived up to people's expectations and performed like a leader . . . or so I thought. Each next event at the conference seemed more demanding than I could handle. For four days I would hide during the day from the endless encounters that would take more than I had to give, then show up in the evening with a smile and try to give what I didn't have.

Sue and I knew something was very wrong. I called home to my doctor, a wonderful Christian brother, and shared what I was experiencing—the feelings of fear and anxiety, the dread of meeting with people and of being in public, the panic attacks. He assured me that I was not going to die. I needed to hear that; I was beginning to wonder. He asked me to journal my feelings. This would be new for me, and yet I felt it would be easy—my feelings overwhelmed me. I couldn't miss them.

After the conference we drove to St. Louis to visit our son Jeff, who was in seminary. It was more than I could handle. I needed to hide and be alone. I climbed into bed in the early afternoon. I couldn't do this.

The next day Sue and I were hosting a reception for a significant number of seminarians with backgrounds in The Navigators. All were dear friends and co-laborers. We wanted to communicate our love and affirm their calling to be pastors. The reception was both wonderful and horribly hard. It was good to affirm their callings. It was good to bless them. But with every blessing I was giving what I did not have. "It is one thing to be empty," Macrina Wiederkehr writes, "but when you are asked to feed someone out of your emptiness it can be terrifying."[1]

The thought of traveling home the next day filled me with fear. Returning the rental car, maneuvering through a large congested airport, cramming my 6'2" frame into a cramped airplane filled with people sitting way too close to me—I wasn't sure I could do it. Knowing I was returning to the solitude and safety of our home in the Colorado forest, however, infused me with enough tooth-clenching determination to press through the anxiety.

Home. A visit to the doctor to share my journal, a little rest after an unusually busy summer and fall, and all should be well. But it wasn't. I got worse—much worse. The panic attacks continued. They seemed like heart attacks. Fear and anxiety were my constant companions. All my thoughts became dark and negative. Every one. I knew I was going to die. I knew I had a brain tumor. I knew I had cancer. And heart trouble. The sense of impending doom was inescapable.

Sue is an extrovert and has a huge circle of friends that often call on the phone. I couldn't deal with it. It was like they were all in our house and crushing in on me. There was no way I could dredge up the courage or resources to talk on the phone. If a visitor came to our door, I hid in the bedroom. It was all way too much.

I couldn't watch TV. A video was unthinkable, requiring emotional responses I did not have. I couldn't read; the newspaper was far too stressful, and even my favorite Louis L'Amour cowboy novels were too much. The Bible? No way.

Driving was out. Being in public was out. Church was out. Ministry was out. It seemed as if all of life was out. "I can't" was my response to everything. I had a total inability to tolerate real or anticipated stress, no energy to respond to any demand. My days consisted of sitting in my favorite chair and trying to survive. The darkness was impenetrable. What was happening to me?

More trips to the doctor. Anti-depressants. Sick leave. Isolation.

After several months, the darkness slowly began to lift and there were minutes of light, of positive thoughts. Maybe there were some good things in the future? Another month passed, and the feelings of dread, fear and anxiety continued to lessen. The old me seemed to be returning in timed increments.

I was still clueless, however, as to what had hurled me into the months of darkness. Well-meaning friends had plenty of ideas. Lack of whole grain. The wrong vitamins. No discipline. Somehow, deep in my spirit I sensed the root was buried in something more serious. Something was there. The Spirit of God was beginning to gently nudge me to take a look.

There was no question I had a serious case of depression. The genetic tendencies are in my family. Yet could this also be a spiritual crisis? Could it be what Saint John of the Cross described in the sixteenth century as a "dark night of the soul"? He described an extended time in which all the spiritual disciplines lose their appeal, a feeling of abandonment by God. In reality, God is busy working deep in the soul. It is a time of God's loving discipline, of healing what is lame "so that what is lame may not be put out of joint but rather be healed" (Hebrews 12:13). Was something lame and deformed in my life?

With periods of normalcy returning and the encouragement of The Navigators' US president, I cranked up the courage to have dinner with a counselor. After I had told him my story, he invited Sue and me to spend a day with him and his wife.

Little did we know that this time with Bill and his wife, Grace, was to be the beginning of the most life-changing relationship we have ever had. They were living a truth that we both desperately needed. They understood the grace of God. They understood the gospel. The environment Bill and Grace created for us in their home was incredibly safe. They listened and asked some gentle questions. Bill's comments were few, but he started wondering with me if there wasn't something out of whack in my relationships that had finally sent me into burnout. He closed our time with a suggestion that would change our lives forever: he proposed that we meet with a trusted friend of his for a counseling intensive.

The Missed Warning Signs

Sue and I had always been leery of counselors; we thought they were only for problem people. But I was willing to do anything to avoid a repeat of what I had just been through. Anything—even going to a counselor. I was an accomplished leader of a national ministry; why was I suddenly so incapable of facing the activities of everyday life?

I had joined the national leadership team of The Navigators a couple of years previous to my burnout and depression. I immediately volunteered to direct our national staff conference, a once-every-four-years event for all our American staff. I had experience directing large conferences, so it was natural for me. The bigger the event, the more I loved it. Cameras, lights, hotels, contracts, staging, speakers, bands—I got to orchestrate and control it all.

Two years of hard work culminated in four energy- and Spirit-filled days in Orlando, Florida—the fun capital of

America. My adrenaline was surging. I was on top of my game, or so I thought. I was completely unaware of the energy I had expended trying to please twelve hundred Navigators staff. It seemed like they all had opinions of how the conference should or should not be run. My reputation was at stake—twelve hundred times over!

Sue and I knew we would be tired after the conference, so we spent the following week vacationing. I was exhausted, but sleep was fitful and shallow. Strange. While driving back to Colorado my mind would jump ahead to student ministry activities scheduled in the next few weeks, and I found myself not wanting to participate. Strange again—I normally loved student ministry events.

After a few days at home I attended a small retreat with our collegiate ministry leaders. Four days with some of my closest staff friends, and yet I did not want to go and didn't know why. Strange.

It got stranger. The first night of the retreat I woke with a jolt at 3:00 a.m. filled with anxious energy—enough to light up half the state. It happened again the next night, and the next, and the next.

After I returned home my disruptive sleep worsened, along with other vague symptoms. We thought I must be more exhausted than we realized. We canceled upcoming ministry trips and substituted a week in the mountains. There was only one trip we did not cancel: the missions conference at our former church. We figured that after a week in the mountains, we should be ready for normal life again.

But there was one problem we were not yet aware of: The issues creating these symptoms were not commitments on my calendar, they were in *me*.

Inability to rest, lack of desire, disrupted sleep, worry, fear—these were like tremors before a big earthquake.

Two Intensive Weeks

After the missions conference and the dark times that followed, after my ability to engage with people gradually returned, we headed to Denver for the "counseling intensive"—whatever that was. How long it would last was uncertain: maybe one week, maybe two weeks, maybe three.

Our counselor was a gifted, godly, grace-filled man. Sue and I met with him every morning for three hours. In the afternoon there were books to read, videos to watch, and other assignments. That was our routine for two weeks.

We quickly learned why it's called an "intensive." Those two weeks were filled with discovery, both incredibly good and horribly bad. It was beautiful; it was ugly. It was deep. It was internal—inside-out kind of stuff. Those two weeks jump-started transformation in our lives. They were the first steps of a long journey of learning to live by the gospel of grace and not our performance.

The first ugly reality that was unearthed was a hurtful and painful lie that had been planted deep within me as a young child and adolescent: the lie that I had less worth and value than everyone else. We began to discover how I subconsciously lived to prove to myself and to others that the lie was not true. But my efforts to disprove the lie did not and could not work. All they did was exhaust me.

The Lie Planted

During high school and college my mom entrusted me with some carefully guarded stories and memories from her growing-up years during the Great Depression. They were not pleasant. As with so many of that generation who lived through the Great Depression, there was deep wounding and scarring. She and her younger brother had been physically abused by her father. As punishment for some infraction he would turn on the gas stove and press their hands against the burner. When she was sixteen, she and her brother ran away from home. To get by she worked as a maid and house cleaner. She cut up cereal boxes to put in her shoes to patch the holes in the soles. Clothes were scarce. So was food.

The sad thing about unhealed wounds and unresolved issues is that we never keep them to ourselves. We may think we do, but we don't. Everyone sees them; they affect everyone around us. And so our unresolved issues pass from generation to generation, mutating as they go. "If we don't learn to transform the pain," Richard Rohr warns, "we'll transfer it."[2]

When I was a preschooler, Mom would take me on the bus to the ghetto. We would spend the morning going from rummage sale to rummage sale, buying clothes for a nickel, or a dime, or a quarter. These rummage sales were often sponsored by churches. I can still see them in my mind: old, narrow ghetto stores with dirty windows and tin ceiling squares half falling down from their high perch, brick walls and bare light bulbs illuminating old church tables piled high with wrinkled old clothes that were never folded, never stacked, just heaped in piles. I hated those rummage sale mornings. Part of my dislike was the boredom of a young boy. But there was more—something that did not feel good about buying used clothes others didn't want.

At the same time, my dad provided well for the family. In a few years we would move to a new home and add an in-ground swimming pool.

In my high-school years clothes were important. They were key to being a part of the "in-crowd." But when I would ask Mom for a particular shirt or jacket or sweater the answer was always "No." The "in" clothes were never on the sale table. I can't remember ever having clothes I really wanted. What were the "in" students thinking of me?

Then I went to college. Being a typical college fresh-man, I always had more important things to attend to than laundry—things like tennis, fraternity rush, panty raids. One fall morning I dragged myself out of bed, showered, and opened my closet to get a clean shirt. There was only one left: my one and only dress shirt. No problem. I was a chemistry major and intended to spend the day in the lab, so I put on my dress shirt, threw my lab coat on over it, and headed for the chemistry building. That night I returned to my dorm room, took off my well stained and acid-eaten lab coat, and noticed a round, crusty brown spot on my dress shirt. I poked it with my finger, and the cloth disintegrated.

My one dress shirt now sported a hole the size of a quarter. Sulfuric acid will do it every time.

To this day I vividly remember going to the JC Penney store in downtown Holland, Michigan, to buy a new dress shirt. One I liked. One I wanted. One that was "in" and would earn my place in the "in" crowd. But I found myself paralyzed in front of the shirt counter, with questions flooding my mind. What would my parents say when I took it home for Christmas? Was I worth having a shirt I liked? Was I worth such an "expensive" shirt?

What was going on in me? Why the paralysis? I was immobilized because I was struggling with a lie. John 8:44 warns us we have an enemy—"the father of lies." His goal is to plant untruths in our lives, and he uses the events of life, the unresolved issues of those around us, the sins of others against us, and our own sins to deposit them in us.

The used and unwanted clothes gave the enemy of my soul the opportunity to whisper in my ear: "Bill, you're only worth five-cent shirts and marked-down sale clothes that no one else wants. You are not worth anything nice. You do not have much value." And so a lie was planted—a lie that would shape how I lived for the next thirty or forty years. It controlled me until it exhausted me, and I woke up in the middle of the night with no reserves left to keep disproving the lie.

We all have one, two, maybe three core lies that the enemy has planted in us. Do you know yours? They are lies about who we are, about our worth, about our identity.

They tell us we are ugly, unwanted, unlovable, broken, dirty. On and on the list goes. What they tell us about ourselves is so painful and embarrassing that we become addicted to hiding, and to proving to ourselves and others that what they say is not true. They are lies that contradict the gospel and what God says about us: that we are worth the death of His son, and that He has created in us a new identity that is good and beautiful—an identity that does not need to be hidden.

Even when we are working hard at following Christ, how we live affirms the lie and denies the gospel. The gospel is theory but not reality for us. So at some point there is no option left but to wonder if the gospel message of being a new creation is really true. After all, the me I live with every day does not seem new or beautiful; it feels ugly, second class, and embarrassing, and it needs to be hidden.

Into the Captivity of Hiding

As a young adolescent, I found the lie of having no worth incredibly painful. I needed a plan to prove it was not true. To eliminate the hurt. Or if the lie was true, at least I needed to fool people. This was going to take some work—a lot of never-ending work, work that would eventually take everything I had and then demand still more.

In their book *The Sacred Romance*, John Eldredge and Brent Curtis write, "We come into the world longing to be special to someone."[3] But it's hard to be special when you know you are flawed. Who would want to be around someone who is defective? "If I am not pursued, it must be because there is something wrong with me, something dark and twisted inside."[4] They go on to identify a core anxiety: "We long to be known and we fear it like nothing else. Most people live with a subtle dread that one day they will be discovered for what they really are and the world will be appalled."[5]

I desperately needed a plan to hide my worthlessness. I needed to hide it from myself to anesthetize the pain; I needed to hide it from others so they would believe I had some value. The strategy that subtly took shape was that I would *figure out everyone's expectations of me*, and I would *meet and surpass every one*. I would be everything people wanted and approved of.

Little did I know it would lead me straight into captivity, the captivity of being a people-pleaser.

Performance expectations were suddenly everywhere. There were acceptable grades in school. There were acceptable majors in college. Excellence was always the standard. Every swing needed to be a home run.

After I joined the staff of The Navigators, I felt the added pressure of ministry expectations. How large and fruitful did our campus ministry have to be so that I would be accepted and valued? It probably needed to be bigger, and I probably needed to work harder.

As I moved into leadership roles the number of people I had to please increased exponentially. The higher the leadership positions, the more crushing the expectations. Were my decisions pleasing those I led? Was I heading in the direction *they* would head? Was I friendly enough? Too forceful? What in the world were their expectations? Why couldn't they be easier to figure out?

Then there were our financial supporters to please. How would they react to my buying a car? New or used? Would a Toyota be extravagant? What size house is acceptable? Could I buy a table saw? Is a vacation okay or does it communicate that I am lazy and not working very hard? One week? Two weeks? Where's the line?

These questions exposed my performance addiction. Whenever we hide what we consider to be wrong and worthless in us, we are in captivity. Always. And it's a captivity we cannot escape by working harder to hide our flaws. We are held captive to what we sense are the expectations, standards, and values of others. (I use the word *sense* very deliberately as I discovered later that what I sensed and what was reality were two different things.) Curtis and Eldredge describe this as "living out of a script that someone else has written for us."[6] My problem was that I wasn't held captive by just one person's script; I was held captive by *hundreds* of scripts. I was trying hard to be what I thought I was not.

But captivity runs deeper than being held hostage by other people's scripts. We are also captive to lies that guide our behavior. Lies that determine our relationships, shape our decisions, and form our reactions. These lies hold us tight. No matter how hard we work at proving that the lies are not true, we stay stuck in their grasp.

To put it bluntly, when we allow our lives to be shaped by lies rather than the truth, we are in the captivity of sin. Sin is our master. We are its slave.

Whatever we hide is never healed. Brennan Manning writes, "If we conceal our wounds out of fear and shame, our inner darkness can neither be illuminated nor become a light for others."[7]

And as long as I try to fool others by my behavior so I can hide the "real ugly and worthless" me, I will always be a lonely and unloved person. All another person can love is my mask, my performance. If they begin to see behind the mask, I drive them back by getting angry, by disappointing them, maybe by pointing out the speck in their eye (Matthew 7:3-5). My lie tells me that if they get close enough to see the real me, they will reject me.

Now I am not only unloved and lonely, unable to develop close and intimate relationships, but fear becomes my daily companion—in all my relationships and in all my undertakings. I live in dread of people discovering the real me. What if my friends get too close? What if I blow it in school or miss a quota at work? What if people see I am really a failure? What if . . . ? What if . . . ? What if . . . ?

I was captive to my perception of other's expectations. I was incarcerated in the grip of sin by living out of untruth. In my hiding I was confined to a place where I could not heal. I was enslaved to being unloved and lonely.

Discovering the destructive impacts of my defining lie was very painful. At the same time, thanks to the insights I was gaining through the counseling process, I was discovering a longing to be free. And God was beginning to break through with glimpses of how the gospel had *already* set me free.

This is the message of the rest of the book. But first a little more story.

CHAPTER 2

Glimpses of Freedom

SUE AND I were settling into the counselor's office for another day of our intensive when Milt, our counselor, announced he wanted to talk with me alone that day. Three hours and just me? I could feel my apprehension increasing.

Milt asked me to sit in the leather easy chair and close my eyes. Then he started me on an imaginary journey. He asked me to picture a small theater where I was the only one present. He asked me to put a picture on the screen of myself at a young age and describe it to him. Then another picture, and another, and another. Picture by picture we traveled through my childhood up to my high school years.

Then Milt asked me to select one word to put on the screen. I was not to tell him the word.

I heard Milt's pencil scratching on his legal pad as a word instantly flashed in my mind: *freedom*. We finished the imaginary road trip, and he asked me what word I had put on the screen. After I told him, he turned his pad so I could see it. Written across it in big capital letters was the word *FREEDOM*.

This was quite unnerving, but together we began to probe the idea of freedom. This was dangerous turf for me. Freedom was threatening. I had scripts I had to live out.

Milt explained that every picture I placed on the screen was of me away from home. Walking home from school and picking an apple from the farmer's orchard. Long bike rides. Tennis with my friends at the park by the lake. Always away from home. Always feeling free. You see, my home was not a place of freedom, it was a place of continually asking permission.

As Milt and I processed, it also became apparent that continually having to prove my worth by meeting everyone's expectations led to a continual sense of enslavement. I was captive to being a people pleaser. It was safer to please people and be a slave than allow them to see the "real" me. I was very unfree.

But there was something deeper, something more foundational. Was it okay to be free? Or were these longings for freedom simply the desires of a rebellious heart? Could I be a godly man and be a free man?

And then my core lie kicked in. Did I deserve freedom? Was I worth it? Was I free to spend money on a hobby and not feel guilty? Free to enjoy a vacation? Go to a movie? Have fun? What would people think? Would they be displeased? Would they reject me? Living in freedom threatened my lifelong strategy of having worth and being accepted. *Freedom would change everything.*

Three Glimpses of Freedom

Freedom was scary, but I desperately needed it. My strategy to avoid pain and be significant had led to captivity, exhaustion, burnout, depression, and a year's sick leave. The past year had been a torturous journey through the "dark night of the soul." It felt as if God had abandoned me.

But now, at just the right time, the light of God's truth began to pierce the darkness. In His faithfulness He had always been there, working deeply in my soul, planting new seeds of gospel truth that would grow and enable me to discover and live in gospel freedom.

My first glimpse of freedom was when I realized that *the gospel of grace always eliminates performance as the basis of relationship.* If the basis of my relationship with my Father in heaven is my behavior, my performance, and my trying hard to please Him, then I am not living under grace. I am living under law—the presumption that God's opinion of me is based on my performance—rather than the good news of the gospel, which is that the basis of my relationship with God and His relationship with me is the life and death of Christ. (We will take an in-depth look at this later.)

A principle I don't like, but which is nevertheless true,

is that what is true in our relationships with one another reflects what is true in our relationship with God. How we treat people is always a commentary on our experience with God (1 John 4:20). My strategy of winning people's approval and affirmation by pleasing them reflected my relationship with God. I was on an endless treadmill of trying to be good enough so that God would think well of me. There was no off switch. There couldn't be. People pleasers have never discovered that the gospel sets us free from performance as the basis of our relationship with others and with God.

The second glimpse of freedom occurred when I realized the freedom of *being a new creation in Christ*. Perhaps I wasn't listening when I went to church regularly as a child, but I don't remember hearing the gospel. Not till my freshman year in college, when a classmate involved with The Navigators shared the gospel with me, did I trust Christ. Immediately I had a hunger for God's Word and started memorizing it.[1] I was drawn to Jeremiah 17:9:

> The heart is deceitful above all things,
>   and desperately corrupt;
>   who can understand it? (RSV)

It became my identity and template for living. It told me I had a heart that was evil. I couldn't trust it and following its desires it would corrupt me. The longings of my heart were not safe. Deny them!

I wish I had never memorized it.

It would be years later when one afternoon, as I was processing a counseling intensive assignment, a life-changing truth broke through. Jeremiah 17:9 is no longer true of me as a believer! God had given me a new heart. I am a new creation. I have a new nature that Paul describes as being "created after the likeness of God" (Ephesians 4:24). I don't have an evil heart; I have a good heart.

Could this mean that the desires of my heart were not bad? That they reflected God's desires for me? Could I be free to follow my heart? This was new territory. (We'll unpack this in more depth later.)

My third glimpse of freedom came when I realized *my worth is not anchored in how I please people*. With a bright new freshness I realized my worth is in being the beloved child of God. It is rooted in a Father-child relationship.

The truth of 1 John 3:1—"How great is the love the Father has lavished on us, that we should be called children of God! And that is what we are!" (NIV)—replaced the lie that if I was going to have any worth at all it would take a lot of hard work and someone else's approval. I needed to learn that we don't find our worth in the fruit of our efforts; rather we discover it in becoming God's beloved child. It is our gospel-given-worth that sets us free.

Three Miracles of the Gospel

These three initial glimpses into the freedom that is mine launched me on an incredible journey of unpacking and *experiencing* the gospel. This journey changes everything. It involves learning to trust what God says about my not need-ing to perform to please Him, to trust what He says about my new heart, and to trust that my worth as His child is true.

Each of these three glimpses of freedom is anchored in a unique aspect of the gospel. The gospel is not one isolated act of God. It's not one piece of good news. The gospel is multifaceted, and embedded in its good news are multiple miracles, which set us free and transform us as we learn to trust them.

Too often we reduce the gospel to something much smaller and less transforming than it is. When we do this we forfeit the freedom Christ died to give us.

In the rest of this book we will look at each of these three unique aspects of the gospel and explore how they set us free. But first let me summarize them and offer some context for each.

The first unique aspect of the gospel is that *God views me differently*. He sees Jesus' obedience as mine; He sees Jesus' punishment for sin as mine; and so He declares me to be righteous as Jesus is righteous. God is always looking at me through the lens of the life and death of Christ. Theologians call this God's imputed righteousness.

If our understanding of the gospel ends here, however, we have an incomplete and ineffective model of how to mature as a believer. Sin will continue to master us—no matter how often we remind ourselves and how thankful we may be for this miraculous work of God.

The second miracle of the gospel is that *God also makes me different*. I am a new creation. I have a new nature. I am not who I used to be. It is this miracle of the gospel that allows me to mature and grow in Christlikeness. It allows me to stop the relentless effort of trying to become someone different as the pathway to holiness and pleasing God. God has already made me different. He has done it for me.

The third miracle of the gospel is that *God relates to me differently*. God changes from being my judge to being my father, and I change from a being a guilt-burdened orphan to being His forgiven and loved child. Unfortunately many Christians live in daily fear of God as their judge. The fear of God's punishment motivates them to obey—but it doesn't work. Thankfully the gospel changes all of this. The freedom embedded in this good news runs deep.

God views me differently. God makes me different. God relates to me differently. It is in these three miracles of the gospel that we find our freedom and transformation.

PART ONE

GOD VIEWS ME DIFFERENTLY

CHAPTER 3

Miracle One:
The Unconditional
Good News

BEFORE WE DISCOVER the way to a relationship with God through faith in Christ (rather than through our behavior and trying to be good enough to please Him), we are stopped dead in our tracks with a double dilemma—a relational predicament and a punishment problem. But before looking at this double dilemma—and its solution—let's look at how we get ourselves in this quandary.

Sin and Law
The strategy of pleasing God by performance is what the Scriptures call living "under the law." The term *law* refers both to the Old Testament law and to its underlying principle: of attempting to please God by our discipline, by our obedience,

29

by our hard work and tireless effort, by bucking up and show-ing God we really mean it this time. Trying to gain God's approval and acceptance by our behavior is sweaty, hard work!

The problem of pleasing God by our behavior and keep-ing the law is it does not work (Romans 8:3). The apostle Paul teaches that "those who are in the flesh *cannot please God*" (Romans 8:8; emphasis added). Before we trust Christ and receive a new nature, all we have is life in the flesh (John 3:6). So no matter how hard we try to please God, we are doomed to fail.

In his letter to the Galatians, Paul gives personal testi-mony about how well law-keeping and behavior modifica-tion worked for him. "I tried keeping rules and working my head off to please God, and it didn't work" (Galatians 2:19, MSG). Everyone, he reminds them, who bases their relation-ship with God on law-keeping and be-good conduct is "under a curse." But the good news is that "Christ redeemed us from the curse of the law" (3:10, 13).

In his letter to the Romans Paul declares that all who base their relationship with God on keeping the law are slaves of sin (Romans 6:14). Attempts to be godly by focusing on law keeping, in reality, keep people enslaved to the sin they are trying to avoid! (This is true for the unbeliever and the believer.) Romans 8:2 describes the law not as the law of holi-ness and godliness but as "the law of sin and death," because the Old Testament law was not able to make us godly; it was not able to make us holy or righteous. The law tells us right things to do, but it never gives the power to do them. We are commanded, for example, to love our neighbor, but the law does not enable us to do so.

So why was the law given? The law fulfills two purposes. First, it reveals our unacceptability to God. It exposes our sin and our unrighteousness. Second, because of what it reveals about us, it leads us to faith in Christ (Galatians 3:24).

First John 3:4 describes sin as "lawlessness"; our inability to keep the law is sin. But our sinfulness runs deeper than our law-breaking *behavior*. We inherited a sinful nature because of Adam's sin. Thanks, Adam! Theologians call this "original sin." The psalmist David acknowledged original sin with these words:

> For I was born a sinner—
>> yes, from the moment my mother conceived me.
>> (Psalm 51:5, NLT)

He reiterates this in Psalm 58:3:

> These wicked people are born sinners;
>> even from birth they have lied and gone their own
>> way. (NLT)

People do not have to be taught to lie, to break the law, or to go "their own way." It comes naturally.

Actually, our sin problem goes back farther than our birth. David said he had a sin problem "from the moment my mother conceived me." Paul describes both his Ephesian friends and himself before coming to Christ as having "lived in the passions of our flesh, carrying out the desires of the body and the mind, and were *by nature* children of wrath" (Ephesians 2:3; emphasis added). We don't just have actions that are sinful; we also have a nature that is sinful. Trying to change our nature poses a huge problem.

The Double Dilemma of Sin

The undeniable fact that we are sinners, by our actions and our nature, creates two problems—a double dilemma, both of which are results of our sin and are problems we are unable to solve.

The first problem is one of *relationship*. Our sin alienates us relationally from God. "Because of your sins, he has turned away and will not listen anymore" (Isaiah 59:2, NLT). We need to be relationally reconciled, relationally reconnected.

Our alienation comes from the fact that our sin is incompatible with God's holiness. The prophet Habakkuk writes that God in His holiness cannot look on sin, and so He must turn Himself away from us (Habakkuk 1:13). But our dilemma is worse than just being disconnected friends that need our relationship repaired; Romans 5:10 refers to us as *enemies* that need reconciliation.

Our second problem is that God takes sin seriously and it arouses His wrath. God's wrath is His holiness reacting to and opposing sin. New Testament scholar Leon Morris writes that God's wrath is His "personal divine revulsion to evil" and His "vigorous opposition to it."[1] "God's wrath," theologian Wayne Grudem tells us, "means that he intensely hates all sin."[2] Like mine. Like yours.

Being punished by God for our sin is not the equivalent of getting a speeding ticket when we add 20 mph to the speed limit. It's not like getting after-school detention for texting in class. It's not even like receiving a prison sentence for some serious crime. These are simply consequences. Romans 6:23 informs us that the "wages of sin is death." The Bible doesn't view death as the natural end of life, but as a *penal* or punitive event.[3] It is the punishment for our sin.

And so our sin creates a double dilemma—alienation and punishment. They are dilemmas because we can do nothing about them. The more we try, the worse it gets and the more evidence there is against us.

The Dilemma Resolved

"With the arrival of Jesus," however, "that fateful dilemma is resolved" (Romans 8:1, MSG). What we could not do, Jesus does for us. How this double dilemma is resolved is one of the miracles of the gospel (but only one).[4]

What did Jesus do? We had two problems, so Jesus did two things.

First, *He obeyed in our place.* While we desperately need the forgiveness of our sins, it is not adequate to overcome our alienation. Forgiveness leaves us in a neutral state of being— not good and not bad. We need God to see us as righteous; then the righteous God can fellowship with righteous man. Alienation resolved.

How do we achieve this righteousness? Romans 3:22 gives us the good news that there is a righteousness from God that can be ours through faith in Jesus Christ. How? It starts with the obedience of Jesus: "By the one man's obedience the many will be made righteous" (Romans 5:19). As believers, we are "the many"!

When we put our trust in Christ, one of the things we are doing is trusting in "the one man's obedience" as the basis of our relationship with God, rather than our own behavior. Then God does a miraculous thing—He thinks of Christ's righteousness, His obedience, as ours! Christ's righteousness is imputed, or credited, to us.

Second, *Jesus took our punishment for us.* The second part of our dilemma, God's punishment for our sin, is solved by trusting in Christ's death on the cross. First John 2:2 teaches, "He is the propitiation for our sins." *Propitiation* is an unusual word, and understanding it is important. John Stott says that "to 'propitiate' somebody means to appease or pacify their anger."[5] Jesus, by His death on the cross, turned aside the wrath of God from us by absorbing it in our place. Jesus substituted for us. He took our penalty and died our death. The prophet Isaiah vividly prophesied this:

But it was our sins that did that to him,
    that ripped and tore and crushed him—*our sins!*
He took the punishment, and that made us whole.
    Through his bruises we get healed. (Isaiah 53:5, MSG)

When we put our faith in Christ, we are trusting in His obedience and trusting in His punishment as the basis of our relationship with God—no longer are we trusting in our behavior. That was a dead-end street. Brennan Manning writes, "The foremost characteristic of living by grace is trust in the redeeming work of Jesus Christ."[6]

The New Testament uses the words *justify* and *justification* to describe God's response to our trust. Romans 3:26 (NIV) says that God is "the one who justifies those who have faith in Jesus." The New Living Translation puts it this way: "He declares sinners to be right in his sight when they believe in Jesus." So to be justified is to be declared to be right, to be righteous. God does this because He views us through the life and death of Christ. He sees us as obedient. He sees our sin as having been punished. He no longer sees us as law-breakers. God counts Christ's righteousness as ours and therefore makes a declaration about us—we are righteous! G. K. Chesterton called this miracle "the furious love of God."[7]

In his classic book *The Cross of Christ* John Stott describes this first miracle of the gospel, our *imputed righteousness*, this way:

> When we are united with Christ a mysterious
> exchange takes place: he took our curse, so that we
> may receive his blessing; he became our sin, so that
> we may become righteous with his righteousness.
> Elsewhere Paul writes of this transfer in terms of

"imputation." On the one hand, God declines to "impute" our sins to us, or "count" then against us (2 Cor 5:19), with the implication that he imputed them to Christ instead. On the other, God has imputed Christ's righteousness to us (Romans 4:6; 1 Cor 1:30; Phil 3:9).[8]

Saint Athanasius called this "the great exchange."[9] God relates to us as righteous. He no longer relates to us based on *our* behavior! The implications of this and the freedoms it provides are life-changing; if we have not experienced them as such, we may know the gospel in our heads, but we are not experiencing it. We will explore these freedoms in the rest of Part One.

Justification is a declaration of how God views us. As Wayne Grudem reminds us, it "does not change our internal nature or character at all."[10] Changing us from the inside takes a second miracle of the gospel; we will look at that in Part Two.

When we decide to "become a Christian" it looks like this:

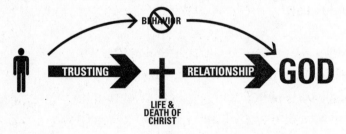

We are now trusting in the obedient life of Christ and the death of Christ as the basis of our relationship with God. *Never again do we trust in our behavior as the basis of that relationship.*

But there is more. Just as *I* trust in the life and death of Christ as the basis of my relationship with God, so *God* depends on the life and death of Christ as the basis of his relationship with me. Never again does my relationship with God depend on my behavior. Now the diagram looks like this:

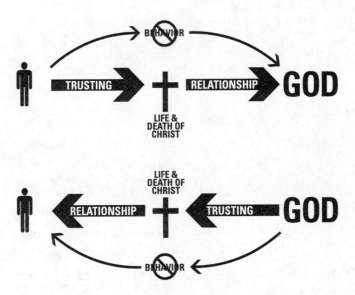

Whether it is us relating to God or God relating to us, the foundation of the relationship is always the grace of God as experienced in the obedience and death of Jesus.

Set Free from Performing

The truth that *the gospel eliminates performance as the basis of relationship* gave me the first initial glimpse of the freedom that was mine. I could stop *trying* to be acceptable to God because I already was! I could stop trying to perform my way to intimacy with God. My intimacy is based on the behavior of Christ. God is looking at me through Christ, sees me as righteous, and is already pleased with me! Every day, 24/7. C. S. Lewis argued that how God thinks of us is "not only more important, but infinitely more important," than how we think of God.[11]

This truth got me off the endless exhausting treadmill of trying to please God by my efforts, my discipline, my faithfulness, and all the other ways I was trying so hard to please him.

If I assume God is more pleased with me some days than others, if I believe He is still relating to me based on my behavior, then I'm saying that the life and death of Christ is not enough. To believe this is to deny the gospel.

Does the truth that God's relationship with us is based on the gospel and not our behavior give us permission to sin, to live a sloppy Christian life? Of course not! The miracle of the gospel never inflames the heart of the believer to sin. Tim Keller suggests that the gospel actually "devours the very motivation you have for sin."[12] The gospel gives us a new heart, a heart that does not want to sin. (We'll discuss this further in Part Two.)

Set Free by Jesus

Jesus says that "the truth will set you free" (John 8:32). What's the truth that sets us free? A lot of colleges and universities think it's their curriculum; they have chosen these words of Jesus as their motto and have it engraved above their libraries' entrances. Many journalists think the freedom of the press sets us free. Some counselors argue that discovering and understanding our wounded past sets us free. For others it is positive self-talk that is freeing.

They are all wrong; they stopped reading too soon. Four verses later Jesus says "the Son sets you free" (John 8:36). The truth that sets us free is not personal insight, not a set of statements, not time-honored principles, not even Bible verses; the truth that sets us free is the person Jesus. Jesus makes this clear again in John 14:6: "I am . . . the truth." For believers, truth is not an *it* but a *who*—and the *who* is Jesus. Jesus, and His work on our behalf, is the only path to freedom.

Our freedom is incredibly important to Jesus. He died for it. But He died for more than just freedom *from* something; he died *for* something. "For freedom Christ has set us free" (Galatians 5:1). We have been set free from all that holds us captive so that we can live every day *in freedom*. It can be a continual reality.

Let's look at the ways this first miracle of the gospel sets us free.

CHAPTER 4

Free from Performing for Love and Relationship

DOES MY BEHAVIOR affect how close God and I are in this gospel relationship? Can I work on our relationship so we are closer, more intimate? Is it my responsibility to draw near to God so He will draw near to me? Does my disobedience and sin create a distance between God and me?

To answer these questions we need to expose two lies that pervade Christendom. The first lie is that it is our responsibility as believers to live in such a way that God is pleased with us. To debunk this lie we will look at Jesus' words in John 15 about the connection between our obedience and God's relationship to us.

The second lie is the flip side of the first one: We are

responsible to repair the relational distance between us and God created by our sin. Our sin makes God displeased with us, causing Him to love us less and creating a relational distance between us that we are responsible to repair. To expose this lie we'll take a look at key gospel truths in Romans and 1 John.

Two inseparable lies. To believe one is to believe the other. To believe them creates a joyless, exhausting, anti-gospel life. For me, believing these lies led to burnout and depression.

The First Lie: Our Obedience Unlocks God's Love

The good news of the gospel is that God's love for us is unconditional. Always. At least we know this in our *heads*. The problem is, we *live* as if it is not true. And then we disciple the next generation to live as if it's not true.

When we live contrary to God's unconditional love and pass on this way of living to the next generation, Satan is ecstatic. Why? He has won. Our lives are denying gospel reality. We are living like Jesus never obeyed and died in our place. We live as though we are still under the law—still needing to perform for God's approval. Then we recruit others to live in the same way.

How do we live as though God's unconditional love for us is not true? We relegate His unconditional love for us to a single point in time in the past: when we became a Christian. Ah yes, His unconditional love was the source of my salvation. But if I want to *continue* to receive His love and acceptance I need to perform, obey, be faithful, not sin, be holy, be disciplined, memorize Scripture, attend church no matter how bad the weather, and obey the Beatitudes!

Wrong! A relationship tied to our performance, whether good or bad, is still a conditional relationship—not a gospel relationship. Milton Vincent writes of "the costly mistake made by Christians who view the gospel as something that has fully served out its purpose the moment they believed in Jesus for salvation. Not knowing what to do with the gospel once they are saved, they lay it aside."[1] When we lay aside the gospel, we lay aside the experience of God's unconditional love for us.

The gospel means God's love for us is unconditional *today*. The intimacy of our relationship with God is disconnected from our performance. Let's explore this in John 15:9-12.

I Will Prove That I Love God!

John 14–15 unfolds the connection between our obedience and God's love for us. For years I didn't enjoy these chapters; they smacked of a lot of hard work on my part. It was difficult reading them without feeling like a failure. I read these verses as commands to obey so I could show God I loved Him; then He would love me back. But what if they aren't commands but rather *identity verses*—verses that describe our new life in Christ?

John 14:15—"If you love me, you will keep my commandments"—is a good example of how I misunderstood Jesus' words and turned good news into bad news. I heard it like this:

If you love me, you will prove it to me by keeping my
commandments and obeying.

There was my day's task list: to prove my love for God. I
not only had to keep His commands to not sin, I also had to
keep all the positive ones: be loving, be kind, be patient, be
generous . . . the list was endless. Yep—this is what 1 John
5:3 tells me: "For this is the love of God, that we keep his
commandments." So get busy, Bill!

All this made sense to me, except for the very next phrase:
"*And his commandments are not burdensome*" (1 John 5:3;
emphasis added). Are you kidding me? The commandments
of God make up quite a formidable list!

But what if in these verses Jesus is not telling us to do
something, but rather is describing us? What if He is saying,

Since you are somebody who already loves me because of
what I have done in you, you know what you will want
to do? You will want to keep my commandments. That's
what you are like. That's you.

The word *if* is not always conditional, as in "I will do this
if (and only if) you do that." It can also refer to a presup-
position or condition: "If x is true, then it follows that y is
also true." In such cases *if* is perhaps more helpfully rendered
as *since*.

In this instance *if* is more declarative than conditional.
Jesus shares the incredible good news of the gospel with us,

that we love God because God first loves us (1 John 4:19). As part of His miraculous love, He gives us a new nature that wants to obey Him. That's the new us.

Another discouraging verse for me was John 14:21:

Whoever has my commandments and keeps them, he it is who loves me. And he who loves me will be loved by my Father, and I will love him and manifest myself to him.

Through my performance filters I heard Jesus saying, *"You need to obey to show God you love Him so that He will be pleased with you and will love you back."* We know this can't be what He means, however, because it makes His love for us *dependent* upon our love for Him. It makes us the initiator in our relationship; it puts our love first and God's love second.

This is backward. It is the gospel reversed from good news to bad news. John Calvin calls such a thought "absurd": "There is no ground for the inference, that the love with which we love Christ comes in order before the love which God has toward us."[2]

But again, what if this is not a *commandment* verse but an *identity* verse—a verse describing us? What if Jesus is saying something like this:

Since you love me because I first loved you and have done all kinds of great things in you, you are that person who keeps my commands. My new creation in you is

*the source of your obedience. Don't ever think it is your
obedience that proves your love for me. And don't ever
think it is your love for me that makes me love you.
You love me because I have loved you. Always have
and always will. Same with my Father. And in this
incredible relationship of ours, you will experience me
up close and in person. That's a promise; I will make
sure it happens.*

Now His command is not burdensome, and the gospel is
good news!

One Thing Jesus Can't Do, and One Thing I Can't Do
That's the lead-up to Jesus' words in John 15:9-12. First He
says, "As the Father has loved me . . ." The English language
has difficulty with the verb "has loved." In English, we use
verb tense to refer primarily to the *time* of action. In Greek,
the verb tense refers primarily to the *kind of action*. The *aorist* tense in this passage refers to action that happened and
finished in the past. Jesus is saying that His Father's love for
Him is complete. It is a done deal.[3]

Since the beginning of time, there is nothing Jesus can do
to make His Father love Him more (see John 17:24). Jesus'
obedience did not cause God the Father to love Him more.
God's love for Jesus was complete.

Jesus continues: "As the Father has loved me, so have I
loved you" (John 15:9). The verb that describes Jesus' love
for us is again in the aorist tense; Jesus is telling us His love

for us is 100 percent complete. There is nothing we can do to make God love us more than He already does in Christ Jesus. Nothing! No amount of effort can make Him love us more.

But there is more good news buried in this verse: Jesus' love for us is in direct proportion to the Father's love for Him! (See John 17:23). God does not motivate us to get with His program by withholding a portion of His love. God's love and acceptance is not a carrot dangling in front of us to motivate us to keep making progress.

This is where our theology and the reality of our Christian living hit a fork in the road. Too many of us, Lloyd Ogilvie explains, "try to live so that he will love us, rather than living because he has already loved us."[4] We boldly teach God's unconditional love, and then live and coach others to live as though His love for us is dependent on our faithfulness, our discipline, our sinlessness, our relentless efforts to please Him. We exhaust ourselves trying to live up to a standard that will enable God to be pleased with us and love us. I know. I tried it. Then we impose this standard on others and they too become exhausted and feel like failures every day. I did that too.

The reality is that God's unconditional complete love was not just true at the point in the past when we trusted Christ. It is still true today! And because it is true today, it should radically affect how we live and enjoy our relationship with God. God is not relating to you on the basis of your behavior. He does not love you more because you obeyed; He does not love you less because you disobeyed. He does not love you more when you resist temptation; He does not love you less if you give in to temptation. *"God loves you,"* Brennan Manning assures us, *"just as you are and not as you should be."*[5]

You can step off your treadmill of trying to please God. His love for you right now is 100 percent complete. There is no percentage left to earn. Today, regardless of how successful or unsuccessful you feel you have been in living your new life in Christ, God is head-over-heels in love with you.

So Why Obey?

In John 15:9, right after Jesus says His love for us is complete, He encourages His disciples to "abide in my love." Evidently, though God's love for us is complete and there is nothing we can do to earn more of it, we are somehow able to move in and out of our *experience* of it.

Sue and I have an exercise bike in our basement. It is totally paid for. It is completely ours. There is nothing we can do to increase our ownership of it. Unfortunately, our *experience* of the bike has been sporadic! So it can be with God's love for us: It's ours, but we may not be experiencing it.

Jesus telling us to remain in His love communicates some responsibility to us. Thankfully, He does not leave us clueless as to what this responsibility is. In verse 10, He tells us the key to experiencing His love: "If you keep my commands, you will abide in my love." This is an incredibly significant statement, as it clarifies *the purpose of obedience.*

We do not obey so that God will love us. He already loves

us fully. *We obey so we can experience the love He already has for us.* What a radical reversal this is from how we so often read the Scriptures and how we live. God's love is not for us to *earn*. It is for us, as believers in God, to *experience*.

There Is No Joy in Effort

We can't stop looking at John 15 quite yet, or we miss a profound truth and the reason Jesus has said all this. Why did Jesus clarify the relationship between our obedience and His love for us? In John 15:11 He says this: "These things I have spoken to you, that my joy may be in you, and that your joy may be full." *The Message* translates this as, "I've told you these things for a purpose."

Thomas Aquinas wrote, "No man can live without joy." We desperately need the joy that is ours in Jesus. In the absence of that joy, we look for cheap substitutes in the wrong places. Aquinas continued, "one deprived of spiritual joy goes over to carnal pleasures."[6]

If joy were a result of our efforts to persuade God to love us by our obedience, there would simply be no joy. Ever. Every night we would ask ourselves if we have done enough for God to be wildly in love with us, and every night the answer would be *no*. The next day we would try harder, we would ask the same question, and we would get the same answer. On and on we would go until we crashed or decided it's impossible and simply quit. Maybe we would still put on a show in public, but on the inside the joy tank would be empty if our joy were contingent on our ability to make God love us.

Leslie Weatherhead wrote that "the opposite of joy is not sorrow. It is unbelief."[7] In the gospel, joy is never earned. It is never the result of our effort. It is Jesus' joy, which He gives to us. It's our joy because we experience it.[8] We can end each day filled with joy because God's love for us is totally complete; He is wildly in love with us! Just as we are.

Yeah but . . .

Every time I teach these gospel truths, hands shoot up with a bunch of "yeah buts." We are wise to never accept a teaching that contradicts the gospel. But what about the apparent contradictions *within* the gospel—such as those we've looked at in John 14–15?

When a verse or a passage seems to have a meaning that is contrary to the gospel, we know immediately we don't have the correct understanding. We need to keep studying. An example is John 15:14: "You are my friends if you do what I command you." He seems to contradict what He just said! Immediately we know that our cursory interpretation of it can't be right.

So what does Jesus mean? John Calvin writes, "He does not mean that we obtain so great an honor by our own merit."[9] D. A. Carson clarifies the meaning: "This obedience is not what *makes* them friends; it is what *characterizes* his friends."[10] In other words, friends act like friends. This is consistent with Jesus' earlier teaching that we are friends and obey because of what *God* has done for us and in us. Friendship is a gift of God's grace, not a result of our effort.

"The unearned love of God," Brennan Manning warns us, "can be disturbing."[11] The idea of earning God's love and friendship without work grinds on the very core of our being. It eliminates our ego and pride—our sense of accomplishment. We like getting credit; it highlights our performance. But God's love is not a reward or trophy, it's a gift, based not on our outstanding performance but on Jesus' performance —His life, His death, and His resurrection. It is all grace.

The Second Lie: My Disobedience Distances Me from God
If the first lie keeping us from experiencing freedom and intimacy with God was that my obedience makes God love me, the second lie is the converse: that my disobedience makes God love me less. He is less pleased with me and enjoys me less.

Many followers of Jesus believe that when they sin, their sin comes between them and God. Their intimacy and friendship with God is broken. We may still be God's children, but there is a distance in the relationship. The closeness is gone. After all, this is what the prophet Isaiah tells us:

> Your iniquities have made a separation
> between you and your God. (Isaiah 59:2)

It is true that sin separates and alienates us from God. But the gospel changes everything. Isaiah 59:2 is not true for the believer, the one who trusts Christ for salvation. Our sins do not create distance between us and God that we need to overcome. The only thing between us and God is Jesus!

John Lynch, pastor of Open Door Fellowship in Phoenix, Arizona, and one of the authors of *TrueFaced* and *The Cure*, illustrates it this way. We think that when we sin, our sin is between us and God; He is now way over there, on the far side of this ugly, smelly heap. So we begin to make promises to God: "Just wait, we will be close again . . . Give me a little time . . . I will work on this. You'll see, we'll be friends again." And then we go to work on all the sin that is between us, relentlessly working to get it out of our lives, out from between us and God. It is exhausting work. It takes more discipline and effort than we have, but we really want to be close to God again, so we stay at it. And at it.

Then, just when we think we are making progress, it seems like forty more dump truck loads of sin are dumped between us. More work. Will it ever end?

Lynch suggests this: What if God never moved? What if we didn't move either? What if our sin actually never came between us? What if God is standing alongside of us, not with our sin between us but with His arm tightly around us and our sin out in front of us? And then what if He says He can help us with that sin?

Wow! This changes *everything*. Not only can I stop trying so hard to get God to love me, I can get off of that treadmill of trying to deal with my sin so that we can be close.

Could it be that what God says to us in Romans 8:37-38 is really true? Nothing whatsoever "will be able to separate us from the love of God in Christ Jesus our Lord." Nothing—not even my sin! *The Message* puts it this way:

> I'm absolutely convinced that nothing—nothing living or dead, angelic or demonic, today or tomorrow, high or low, thinkable or unthinkable—absolutely *nothing* can get between us and God's love because of the way that Jesus our Master has embraced us.

I love what Paul Tripp says, "In his grace, [God] won't play hide and seek with you."[12]

As Jesus was hanging on the cross experiencing God's wrath for our sins, He cried out with horrible agony, "My God, my God, why have you forsaken me?" (Matthew 27:46). What was going on? Commentator Homer A. Kent, Jr., puts it this way: "God . . . had to be separated from him if he was to experience spiritual death in the place of sinful men."[13] Jesus experienced separation from God so that we would never have to ask God, "Why have you forsaken me—where have you gone?"

Does this mean our sin does not matter to God? Of course not. "God does not condone or sanction evil," Brennan Manning assures us. "But," he goes on, "he does not withhold his love because there is evil in us."[14]

Yeah but . . .

Some people rationalize the second lie by distinguishing between love and fellowship. "It's like a father and a son—when the son disobeys, the father still loves the son, but their fellowship is broken." That may be true of human fathers and sons, but it is not true of the relationship between our heavenly Father and us. When we look at our fallen ways of living life to describe God, he winds up looking just like us. Unfortunately many of us do just that, following Pascal's observation, "God made man in his own image and man returned the compliment."

Irenaeus, an early theologian from the second century AD, wrote extensively to confront heresies about the nature of God that were threatening the young church. He warned that false teachers "ascribe those things which apply to men to the Father. . . . But if they had known the Scriptures, and been taught by the truth, they would have known, beyond doubt, that God is not as men are."[15]

I wonder if Irenaeus was thinking of the book of Hosea. In it God is lamenting His love for Israel. The more He loved and nurtured them, the more they went astray. Their behavior stirred up His anger, but because of who He is, He didn't give up on them. Here is how *The Message* renders this glimpse into our Father's commitment to relationship:

When Israel was only a child, I loved him.
　I called out, "My son!"—called him out of Egypt.
But when others called him,
　he ran off and left me. . . .
But how can I give up on you, Ephraim?
　How can I turn you loose, Israel? . . .

I can't bear to even think such thoughts. . . .
And why? Because I am God and not a human.
(Hosea 11:1-9)

Our fellowship with God is *not* broken when we sin. God has not gone anyplace. He has not moved away. He is there with his arm tightly around us. And we have not gone anyplace either; we remain held tight in His grasp. David journaled that there was no way to put distance between us and the embrace of God:

If I take the wings of the morning
    and dwell in the uttermost parts of the sea,
even there your hand shall lead me,
    and your right hand shall hold me. (Psalm 139:9-10)

For David this was great news. Some of us may see it differently.

But you say something has changed. Yes it has. So, if our fellowship has not changed, what *has* changed? Because we sinned, we are not *enjoying* our fellowship with God. God is light, and our sin would prefer the darkness of distance. We are squirming in His embrace. We feel dirty, unworthy, guilty. We might find ourselves wishing there *were* some distance between us!

But here is the good news. As Brennan Manning writes, "We cannot assume that he feels about us the way we feel about ourselves."[16] When we look at God through our sin, we see Him wrongly.

God's loving embrace reaches past our sins to include our hurts, our disappointments, and our sorrows. Little sends me into a melancholic funk more than being disappointed. When my expectations are not met, I feel as if God has let me down. But still God's goodness has not changed. As C. S. Lewis wrote, "We often, almost sulkily, reject the good God offers us because, at the moment, we expected some other good." God in His love knows what is best for us and keeps us in His loving embrace.

Why Confession?

For years I used 1 John 1:9 to get my sin out from between God and me so that our fellowship could be restored. "If we confess our sins," John writes, "he is faithful and just to forgive us our sins and to cleanse us from all unrighteousness." This was the second verse I memorized as a freshman in college and yet some forty-five years later I found myself unsure of its meaning. I read, I studied, and I researched, but everything seemed to reinforce the idea that God retreats to a safe distance from me. I was repulsive to Him in my sin. It seemed as if he stops looking at me through Christ—until I confess to get my sin out from between God and me so that our fellowship could be restored.

But if our sin doesn't come between us and God, what purpose does confession serve?

One day I focused on the phrase, "He is faithful and just

. . . to *cleanse* us" (emphasis added). Yes! That was what I needed, cleansing. If I stopped feeling dirty, I could stop squirming in God's grip. If I was clean and my guilt was gone, I could enjoy the relationship and the intimate fellowship that I found myself in.

Our confession isn't meant to get our sin out from between God and us. It isn't meant to restore the relationship. Confession is the way God washes us so we can stop being so uncomfortable in our relationship with Him.

Yeah but . . .

Yeah, but what about James 4:8? "Draw near to God, and he will draw near to you." Doesn't this imply our sin has created a distance between us and God? Doesn't it seem as though the responsibility lies with us to close the gap? That we move first and God responds?

John Calvin assures us that "the Apostle meant no such thing."[17] Such an interpretation is contrary to the gospel, so to understand this passage we need to understand the context—both the immediate context in James and, as always, the context of the gospel.

In this passage, James was admonishing some highly dysfunctional Christians. They'd been quarreling, fighting, killing one another with their words, and completely focused on their own desires. They are trapped in a downward spiral of habitual and repetitive sin. James warns them that "friendship with the world is enmity with God" (4:4).

How do they break out of the downward spiral? James

sets the stage: "God opposes the proud, but gives grace to the humble" (4:6). He follows with ten imperatives and concludes with a renewed call to "humble yourselves before the Lord, and he will exalt you" (4:10).

What is humility? Humility is telling God (and others) the truth about what we are really like. We learn this from Jesus' parable of the Pharisee and the tax collector (Luke 18:9-14). They both walk into the Temple to pray, but the Pharisee is anything but humble; he prays and thanks God that he is not like other men who sin. The tax collector, by contrast,

> slumped in the shadows, his face in his hands, not
> daring to look up, [and] said, "God, give mercy.
> Forgive me, a sinner." (v. 13 *The Message*)

The tax collector tells the truth about himself. "God, I'm a sinner, I'm broken, dirty, messed up to my core." He does not hide his sin. He doesn't wear a mask. Humility is incompatible with mask wearing.

Jesus concludes the parable stating that the person who practices humility, like the tax collector, will be healed, restored, and lifted up. God gives grace to the humble.

Back to James. Could it be that drawing near to God is simply the practice of humility? Taking off the masks, telling God what we are really like—stuck in sin, confused, scared, discouraged, whatever. In that humility we discover the grace of God. It's been right there all the time—only a mask away.

The miracle of the gospel is that we do not first have to clean up our act and beat down our sin in order to be close to God. The gospel sets us free to practice mask-free humility without fear, and to enjoy the intimacy that is already ours.

Does this eliminate effort on our part to walk in obedience? No! The issue is which comes first. Obedience doesn't come first and then union and fellowship with God; union and fellowship with God give us the ability to obey with a wholehearted effort. Grace never eliminates effort—it eliminates earning.

Free from Performing for God's Love and Friendship

The first miracle of the gospel is that God views us differently, seeing Jesus' obedience and punishment as ours, and so declaring us to be righteous—the first miracle is God justifying us. Performance has been eliminated as the basis of relationship and fellowship. This sets us free from the grueling pursuit of being good enough to deserve God's love. Our obedience doesn't cause God to love us, and our disobedience doesn't distance Him from us. We are held tightly in His grasp, not because of who we are or what we have done, but because of who He is. "I am lovable," Brennan Manning proclaims, "because He loves me. Period."[18]

How I needed to discover this freedom. It's the foundational good news of the gospel and has had the greatest effect in setting me free from being an addicted people-pleaser. Because performing for God's acceptance is inseparable from performing for people's acceptance (1 John 4:20), there is no other way to be set free.

There are, however, other ways in which this gospel love sets us free. In the next chapter we will discover the good news that God frees us from condemnation.

CHAPTER 5

Free from Condemnation

MOSES CAME DOWN from Mount Sinai after an extended conversation with God, bringing good news for the people of Israel. They were a special and treasured people, set aside by God, who loved them. Moses informs them their special status was not because they were "more in number than any other people" . . . actually, they were "the fewest of all peoples." They were pretty puny and insignificant as a group of people; there wasn't much power or potential in their numbers. So why was God so committed to loving them? Moses said, ". . . it is because the LORD loves you" (Deuteronomy 7:7-8). *The Message* puts it this way:

God wasn't attracted to you and didn't choose you because you were big and important—the fact is, there was almost nothing to you. He did it out of sheer love, keeping the promise he made to your ancestors.

Why did God love them? *Because He loved them!* And so it is with us. God loves us because He loves us. End of story.

This gospel miracle sets us free from performance; it also sets us free from condemnation.

God's Condemnation—Gone

Justification and condemnation are polar opposites. There is no overlap. *Justify* is a legal term meaning "to acquit or find not guilty." To *condemn* a person, by contrast, means "to declare that person guilty."[1] Opposites.

Romans 8:1 boldly states, "There is therefore now no condemnation for those who are in Christ Jesus." As a Christian, you will never hear condemnation from your Father. Never. Do you still sin? Absolutely. Does God condemn you for it? *No!* The Cross worked, and it worked completely. "Whoever believes in him," the gospel declares, "is not condemned" (John 3:18).

A Declaration of Identity

To be condemned is more than being declared guilty for your behavior; it is to be given a defining identity—an identity based on your behavior. People often give us identities based on our behavior or performance—sometimes it's those closest to us, who love us the most. These labels plant deep roots of shame in us that only the gospel can root out.

A number of years ago I was discipling a young man who had recently been released from the state's juvenile detention center. As a teenager he had been hooked on drugs, and he had resorted to stealing to support his habit. His *behavior* had resulted in a new, unwanted *identity*. Standing before the judge, he likely heard something like this: "You stole (behavior), you *are* a thief (identity)." Not only was he declared guilty of law-breaking behavior, he was condemned as a thief.[2]

Parents often follow the same pattern with their children. A young teen comes home from school with another disappointing grade. Perhaps they got a speeding ticket. I've talked with countless students whose fathers' words still haunt and define them: "You failed again (behavior) . . . you really blew it (behavior) . . . you *are* a failure (identity) . . . you *are* a disappointment (identity)." They were given identities based on their behavior.

You sin, therefore you are a sinner. For those of us who are believers, is this a true statement? The behavioral part is certainly true: we still sin. A lot. The apostle Paul, writing as a mature believer, laments in Romans 7:19 that "I do not do the good I want, but the evil I do not want is what I keep on doing." Likewise, the apostle John wrote, "If we say we have no sin, we deceive ourselves" (1 John 1:8).

But what about the last part of the statement: you sin,

therefore you are a sinner? Is this part true of a follower of Jesus? Dietrich Bonhoeffer writes that "what is worse than doing evil is being evil."[3] Paul openly admitted he still did evil but rejoiced that God did not consider him an evil person. He continues on in Romans 8:1: "There is . . . no condemnation for those who are in Christ Jesus."

This is the absurd and exhilarating good news of the gospel: our identity is no longer based on *our* behavior; it is based on the behavior of *Jesus!* This is why we are called "saints" (for example, Romans 1:7). Our identity is not that of sinners trying hard to become saints. We *are* saints (because of Jesus' behavior) who, like Paul, continue to do things we hate—and sometimes sadly don't hate.

Reading Paul's letters to the early church, it doesn't take long to discover the recipients' behavior is often anything but saintly. But in the gospel *behavior does not create identity.* Never in the New Testament are believers called sinners, even though we see believers sinning. Over sixty times they are called saints.

Yeah but . . .
Yeah, but what about 1 Timothy 1:15, where Paul declares that "Christ Jesus came into the world to save sinners" and confesses that he is the worst, the greatest and the absolute chief of them all—"Public Sinner Number One" (v. 15, *The Message*)? Is this a statement about how Paul views his identity?

Remember, the context determines the meaning. When

Paul says he is the foremost of sinners, he is not referring to his identity but to his former behavior, that he "was a blasphemer, persecutor, and insolent opponent" of the church (v. 13). Continuing on, he says in effect that if Jesus saved Paul, then anyone can be saved.[4] And so "the ultimate sinner became the ultimate saint."[5]

God does not see us as a sinners; He sees us as saints. How, then, do we see ourselves? Do we feel God's attitude toward us changes when we fudge the speed limit, skip a quiet time, hurt our kids with anger, or dwell on something that does not honor Him? Do we feel He would disassociate from such an unfaithful and inconsistent person as us? Does our name tag change from saint to sinner?

In Psalm 73 the psalmist acknowledges that he had a downright bad attitude toward God.

I was brutish and ignorant;
    I was like a beast toward you. (v. 22)

But then he makes this amazing declaration:

Nevertheless, I am continually with you;
    you hold my right hand. (v. 23, emphasis added)

There is no distance, no condemnation; God continues to hold him in His tight embrace. That's the same with us on our worst day. If we are condemned, the Cross did not work. Because the Cross worked, we are not condemned!

> The LORD redeems the life of his servants;
>   none of those who take refuge in him will be
>   condemned. (Psalm 34:22)

Satan's Condemnation—Ignored

God does not condemn us. But we have an enemy who tries to condemn us and resorts to lies. John calls him "the father of lies" (John 8:44). Revelation 12:10 refers to him as "the accuser" of those who call God Father. He stands before God and accuses them "day and night." But his accusations are all lies.

What are these lies that flood the throne of God day and night, that are whispered in our ear and planted in our thinking? They are lies about our identity. They go something like this:

You sinned.

You are guilty.

God knows you are guilty and will remember it.

There is another black mark on your record.

You are a dysfunctional mess, no good whatsoever.

You will never amount to anything.

You will never be faithful in your commitment to God.

You are condemned as a sinner.

So give up. Now.

The accuser—Satan—lies to us about the impact of our sin. He also tells us lies about God—mainly, that His love for us is conditioned on our behavior. Satan makes God out to be a harsh taskmaster and an enemy rather than our friend.

When I feel weighed down by Satan's lies, I often find myself sitting at our piano playing the 1863 hymn *Before the Throne of God Above*.

> *When Satan tempts me to despair and tells me of the guilt within,*
> *Upward I look and see Him there Who made an end to all my sin.*
> *Because the sinless Savior died My sinful soul is counted free.*
> *For God the just is satisfied to look on Him and pardon me.*

Satan tries to condemn us, but he doesn't succeed. God ignores his lies, and so should we.

Our Heart's Condemnation—Overruled

God doesn't condemn us, and Satan tries to but fails. But there is another person who tries to condemn us—we condemn ourselves. As David acknowledged in Psalm 51:5, "I know my transgressions and my sin is ever before me." The memories of our past can haunt us day and night. Often they come flashing back to our minds in 3-D high-definition. Our past is a ball and chain around our ankles—always holding us back, never letting us run unfettered into the future with the lightness of freedom. Others may not see our past or know it is there, but we do. We tug it around every day, and we live in a lonely and secret hiddenness, pretending all is well.

Early in our Navigator career, Sue and I led the Navigator student ministry at the University of Illinois, and I was responsible for training new young staff. Tuesdays I met one-on-one with three men; we would spend time in the Scriptures, praying, talking about ministry, and usually lots more. It was a day I always looked forward to, a day to invest deeply in the next generation of leaders. But one Tuesday my heart screamed condemnation. Tim came first; I had planned to meet in our downstairs family room, but he asked if we could go for a ride instead. Not sure what was up, but confident that if there was a problem it wasn't with me, I said sure. As we drove through the farm country south of the university, Tim sliced through the initial chatter with loving concern: "Bill, what is with you lately? You're cold, unloving, harsh." What I thought was going to be a short ride became much longer.

After lunch I met with Tom. He too gently shared that I had been coming across lately as harsh, insensitive, and unloving—not only to him but to the students on campus. When Tom left I retreated to my study and closed the door. When Sue came to get me for dinner, I was sitting there crying. She assumed my dad had died.

After dinner Geoff, one of the most loving and gentle men I know, arrived for our time together. As we headed down to the family room Geoff asked if we could go back to my study and talk. He closed the door behind us—not a good sign. He proceeded to inquire as to why I was being so unloving, so harsh, so cold . . .

For three days I was in the deepest of dumps. I asked if they had talked to one another and coordinated their conversations. They had not and did not know of the others' intentions. The day had indeed been orchestrated, but by the Holy Spirit, not by them. God was confronting my sin, but my heart was condemning me. I felt my behavior had given me an identity. I didn't just *act* unloving; I had *become* unloving.

To this day I vividly see myself sitting numbly in my study, staring out the window, and periodically glancing at the phone. I wanted to call my supervisor and quit. If I couldn't lead by example, I didn't want to lead.

It's at times like this that the scandalous love of God changes everything. First John 3:20 reminds us that "whenever our heart condemns us, God is greater than our heart, and he knows everything." God knew those three conversations, He knew what I had done, He knew "everything"; and still his commitment to me was "greater" than the power of my sin against Him. When my heart condemns me it means I am giving greater credence to my circumstances and feelings than to what God is saying to me; in His sight my behavior does not create my identity. I am still a saint. I am still free. In those moments we need to believe *God* more than we believe *ourselves*.

Free

Condemnation, whatever the source, is an anchor that holds us in a bad place, filled with lies. Time is not redemptive; I know I am mired in condemnation when the passage of time doesn't set me free.

When I hear Satan whispering, maybe yelling, condemnation in my ear, telling me I have little worth and causing my heart to drag me down with self-condemnation, I need to remember it is all a lie. What God says about me overrules all condemnation from any source. It has the weight of truth. I am free from condemnation. Right now.

CHAPTER 6

Free from Punishment

SINCE GOD DECLARED us "not guilty" and therefore, as believers, not condemned, we will never, never be punished for our sins. *Never!* Not once. Not even a little. Neither will others be punished for our sins.

In Isaiah 53, the great chapter that foretells of Christ's death on a cross some seven hundred years before the actual event, we are told, "My righteous servant will make it possible for many to be counted as righteous, for he will bear *all* their sins" (53:11, NLT; emphasis added). Those who trust Christ will escape punishment, because, as Isaiah puts it, "the *punishment* reconciling us fell on him" (53:5, JB; emphasis added).

The apostle Paul, writing thirty years after Christ's death on the cross, reiterates the same unbelievable gospel truth: "Since, therefore, we have now been justified by his blood, much more shall we be saved by him from the wrath of God" (Romans 5:9). I find many believers live as if Christ's death on the cross is a kind of insurance policy; 80 percent of the costs of their sins is absorbed and covered, but there remains a 20 percent co-pay that they are responsible to cover personally. They are not sure which sins fall into the 20 percent, or how many times they need to commit the same sin before they cross the line, but they anticipate God's punishment.

No! If God still punishes us for our sin—even just some of it—then He is still relating to us on the basis of our behavior and not on the atoning work of Christ. Jesus absorbed the punishment for *all* our sins.

Several years ago I was preaching on this topic in a large church. As Sue and I walked out the front doors to the parking lot after the last service, we overheard an elderly couple evaluating the error of my message with great enthusiasm. The wife said something that sent chills down my spine and I have never forgotten: "If God doesn't punish us for our sins, we will never obey."

The revolutionary good news of the gospel is that God no longer motivates us as believers by the threat of punishment.

Punishment versus Discipline

God never punishes us as believers for our sins; but because of His love for us, He is deeply committed to disciplining us for our sin. Punishment and discipline are very different. They are mutually exclusive and cannot coexist.

God's punishment is rooted in His justice; it is expressed by wrath and anger. This is always God's response when confronted with sin and evil. "For the wrath of God is revealed from heaven against all ungodliness and unrighteousness" (Romans 1:18). Leon Morris describes God's wrath as His "personal divine revulsion to evil" and as His "personal vigorous opposition to it."[1] John Stott writes that if evil "did not provoke him to anger he would forfeit our respect, for he would no longer be God."[2]

Before trusting in Christ's punishment on our behalf, there was no escaping this wrath of God. Paul reminded his fellow saints in Ephesus, "You used to live in sin, just like the rest of the world. . . . All of us used to live that way. . . . By our very nature we were subject to God's anger, just like everyone else" (Ephesians 2:2-3, NLT). God's wrath brought punishment; we are described as "objects of his judgment and . . . fit only for destruction" (Romans 9:22, NLT). The word *destruction* is a semi-nice word for "death"; Paul is more blunt with his Ephesian friends: "Once you were dead because of your disobedience and your many sins" (Ephesians 2:1, NLT). God's punishment always results in death and destruction. The sequence looks like this:

Our Sin → God's Wrath → Punishment → Death

But because Jesus took our sins upon himself and experienced God's wrath and punishment in our place, we are free from God's wrath and subsequent punishment. Jesus "delivers us from the wrath to come" (1 Thessalonians 1:10).

The New Testament is clear. As believers we will not experience the wrath of God and therefore will not experience punishment for our sins. Jesus already made the full payment. Samuel Bolton puts it this way: "It would not be righteous of God to require, nay, to receive full satisfaction of Christ, and to require anything of you."[3] Double punishment is unjust. And so the threat of punishment is never held over our heads as a motivation for obedience.

So how does God respond to our sins? Does He simply ignore them? To do so would be tragic; we would not only continue in them, but our sin would worsen, eventually becoming our master. We can never control sin; thinking we can was the deception of the law (Romans 7:11). Romans 6:19 tells us that sin always leads to *more* sin. And so for God to ignore our sin would be disastrous.

Thankfully God does have a response to our sin. God's *discipline* takes our sin seriously, brings us health, and sets us free from sin's increasing mastery.

Just as God's punishment is rooted in His justice, God's discipline is rooted in His love. "For the Lord disciplines the one he loves" (Hebrews 12:6). When God disciplines us it is always with His loving arms wrapped around us.

If the outcome of God's punishment is our death and destruction, the outcome of God's discipline is our good.

Hebrews 12:10 tells us that God "disciplines us for our good, that we may share his holiness." What a difference! Instead of being angry and punishing us, or just being neutral and ignoring our sins, God loves us *in our sins* and disciplines us so that we may grow increasingly healthy—"so that what is lame may not be put out of joint but rather be healed" (v. 13). While God's discipline may be painful in the moment, "later it yields the peaceful fruit of righteousness" (v. 11).

Discipline looks like this in our lives:

Our sin → God's love → God's discipline → Our holiness, healing, life

The New Living Translation sums it up beautifully: "God's discipline is always right and good for us because it means we will share in his holiness . . . there will be a quiet harvest of right living for those who are trained in this way" (Hebrews 12:10-11, NLT).

Yeah but . . .

What about the last half of Hebrews 12:6: "For the Lord disciplines the one he loves, *and chastises every son whom he receives*" (emphasis added)? Some Bible versions use the word *punishes* in place of *chastises*, making it seem as if God still punishes believers. We know, however, that whatever this word is referring to, it is not punishment for our sins that comes from God's justice, for this would contradict the gospel.

The original Greek word used here for "chastise" is translated elsewhere in the New Testament as "whip" or "flog." It is a translation of a word meaning "to cause pain."[4] The concept of pain in this verse is consistent with the context. Hebrews 12:11 tells us that "for the moment all discipline seems painful rather than pleasant." The difference between the pain of discipline and the pain of punishment is the motive and the outcome. Discipline hurts—it can involve hardship—but, as seventeenth-century Puritan Samuel Bolton wrote, "Afflictions which come upon the godly are medicinal in purpose, and are intended to cure."[5]

When our boys were young they would regularly act quite human for a period of days—argumentative, contrary, pushing the boundaries of our family rules, and just downright disobedient. After a couple of no-fun days of parenting my patience would run out, and the next time one of the boys misbehaved I would ask him to bring me his mom's college sorority paddle. This request always elicited immediate repentance, with weeping and wailing and promises of better behavior in an attempt to forgo the pain of the paddle. After spanking him, I would hold him close and tell him I didn't do it because I was angry but because I loved him. In my heart I knew his future was at stake.

And so it is with God: He disciplines us, and it is painful, but it is born out of His love for us and His desire for our future wholeness.

There are some memorable times I lost my patience and didn't discipline the boys—I reacted to them out of anger and punished them. Knowing I had done wrong, I would confess and ask for forgiveness. I felt terrible for how I acted, but even more for how punishment affected them. It never helped them, and it always strained our relationship. They would immediately respond by stiffening up and drawing away, full of distrust and fear. I remember grabbing David's teenage arm in anger. The more he tried to twist free, the harder I held on. We were in a power struggle. We both lost.

Punishment always plants an increment of destruction and rebellion in the person being punished. It never helps them. They lose. On the other hand, discipline rooted in love has the outcome of healing and health. They win. It is not punishment for the past, it is training for the future. "God is educating you," the writer of the letter to the Hebrews assures us. "That's why you must never drop out. He's treating you as dear children. This trouble you're in isn't punishment, it's training" (Hebrews 12:11-12, MSG).

Discipline is always painful, but it is not the pain of punishment. It doesn't come from impatience, frustration, worry, concern for what others might think, disappointment, annoyance, or anger. It is pain that comes from a concerned and loving heart. Bible translations that use the word *punishment* are using it figuratively as the context of the chapter and the larger context of the gospel demand.[6]

Are Consequences Punishment?

All sin has consequences, and they are always worse than we anticipate. As Reinhold Niebuhr put it, "All human sin seems so much worse in its consequences than in its intention." We see this on the macro level with the sin of Adam, and on the micro level in our own lives. The *intention* of Adam was to simply know good and evil. The *consequences* of his sin in the Garden went far beyond his direct relationships; it had repercussions for the entire human race, and even all of creation was cursed! You and I are still living with the consequences of Adam's sin; creation is still waiting to be redeemed.

We see the consequences of sin in our individual lives and in the lives of those around us. Athletes who use drugs with the intent of winning a game or breaking a record find themselves subjected to congressional hearings, losing their sponsors, making international headlines, and forever being banned from sports. Political candidates drop out because of a moment of indiscretion. Pastors are disgraced. Families are broken. Careers ruined. Health destroyed. Prisons are filled with inmates learning that the consequences of their sin are worse than their intentions.

Before we sin we think that we will be able to control the consequences; after we sin we discover that consequences can never be controlled. We can't control our sin and we can't control its consequences.

The consequences of our sin can be horrific. But for believers, are these consequences God's punishment? The gospel says no. You are impatient or maybe showing off and are driving too fast and slide off an icy road into a tree, wrecking your car, killing a passenger. Is this God's punishment that you will have to live the rest of your life with?

The gospel says no. God is not a spy in the sky watching our every move so He can punish us. He is not our enemy. He is our friend.

Decisions have consequences. Behavior has consequences. Sinful behavior always brings unpleasant consequences, but "none of our sin can bring upon us the consequences of Divine wrath."[7]

Proverbs is a book about consequences, and Proverbs 1:31 offers a good summary of the nature of consequences: "You wanted your own way—now, how do you like it?" (MSG).

Free from Self-Punishment

While attending seminary and helping open a new Navigator student ministry at the University of Kentucky, I accompanied some students on a spring break trip to Mexico City. The city is home to magnificent cathedrals, surrounded by immense public squares paved with stone. I still vividly recall women slowly, painfully, working their way across the square toward the church on their bare knees—punishing themselves and making atonement for their sin by supposedly doing something meritorious.

Like those women, some of us punish ourselves for the sins we commit, sometimes continuing to do so for years. We feel we deserve to be the victim of our sins, to feel bad, to be punished, so we wage war on ourselves, beating ourselves physically, emotionally, and spiritually. We deprive ourselves of newness, of fun, of joy, of relationships, of giving and receiving love, of adventure. We demean ourselves.

Sometimes we try to earn God's love back by doing something meritorious, sacrificial, or heroic.

When we punish ourselves for our sin, we are climbing back on the treadmill of performance. Regardless of whether we feel unworthy of being forgiven and cleansed of the past, *feelings* are not God's criteria for being loved, for being forgiven, or for forgiving ourselves. When we punish ourselves we are rejecting the gospel because we feel *we* need to pay the price for our sin.

Martin Luther, when asked about doing penance as a punishment for sin, is reported to have said, "What is it in our arrogance that makes us think that anything we could ever do would be more sufficient than the blood of God's own son?" The good news is that "the blood of Jesus his Son cleanses us from all sin" (1 John 1:7).

Is Our Death Punishment?

Why do Christians die? Is it because we have sinned? Wayne Grudem summarizes the problem: "It is true that the penalty for sin is death, but the penalty no longer applies to us as believers—not in terms of physical death, and not in terms of spiritual death or separation from God. All of that has been paid for by Christ."[8]

God does not implement all the benefits of salvation at once. In the same way He "has chosen not to remove all the evil from the world immediately, but [to] wait until the final judgment . . . we still live in a fallen world and our experience of salvation is still incomplete."[9] First Corinthians 15:26 tells us that death will be "the last enemy to be destroyed." Until that great day, death remains a reality for us as believers, not as a punishment for our sin but simply as a reality of our living in a fallen world in which all the results of sin have not been completely removed.

But death is more than just an inevitable reality. Samuel Bolton writes, "Death is the godly man's wish, the wicked man's fear."[10] Dietrich Bonhoeffer, before being put to death in a World War II prison camp, called death "the supreme festival on the road to freedom." For Bonhoeffer, freedom was infinitely more than being set free from German captivity, it was the coming experience of the "glorious freedom of the children of God" (Romans 8:21, NIV).

Loved and Free!
For me, performing and punishment were linked. Since God punished, I had to perform—and perform well. Understanding that I am 100 percent free from all punishment has gospelized my obedience; no longer do I obey to please God and so avoid punishment, I obey so I can abide in His love.

Sometimes God's love means discipline, but that is okay. Bryan Chapell writes, "His discipline is never a sign of rejection; it is the mark of your preciousness to God." I am loved. I am precious. And I am free.

Because of the sacrifice of the Messiah, his blood poured out on the altar of the Cross, we're a free

LAY IT DOWN

people—free of penalties and punishments chalked up by all our misdeeds. And not just barely free, either. *Abundantly* free! (Ephesians 1:7, MSG)

CHAPTER 7

Free from Fear

BECAUSE OUR RELATIONSHIP with God is not at risk—our sin not separating us, not condemning us and not causing us to be punished—then we are also set free from *the fear of God*!

Oops. Now I am going too far with this freedom stuff. After all, what about Proverbs 9:10: "The fear of the LORD is the beginning of wisdom?" What about Proverbs 14:27: "The fear of the LORD is a fountain of life?" Even the New Testament seems to encourage us to fear God: "Beloved, let us cleanse ourselves from every defilement of body and spirit, bringing holiness to completion in the fear of God" (2 Corinthians 7:1).

The "Fear-of-the-Lord"

Why would a God who loves us, who delivers us from separation, condemnation and punishment, still require us to fear Him? We need first to recognize the gap between how we hear these words and what they actually mean in the Scriptures. Eugene Peterson, a scholar of ancient languages, observes that we lack "a common and comprehensive term for referring to the way we live the spiritual life, . . . a term that does not make us the center of the subject."

The biblical word of choice for the term we need is "fear-of-the-Lord." It is the stock biblical phrase for the way of life that is lived responsibly and appropriately before who God is, who he is as Father, Son, and Holy Spirit.[1]

The fear-of-the-Lord is how we respond *appropriately* to God as "*Father, Son, and Holy Spirit.*" For believers, this means the work of Christ must be included in our understanding of the fear of God. The biblical term is quite different from how it appears in English. The biblical term "fear-of-the-Lord" is what grammarians call a "bound phrase," or syntagm. An example of a syntagm in English is a sentence, or a paragraph; the meaning of a sentence is not the sum of the meanings of each word in the sentence, rather all the words together create a unique meaning.

In Hebrew "fear-of-the-Lord" is a syntagm: two Hebrew words bound together. We cannot understand the word's meaning by taking the meaning of each individual word and adding them together. If we interpreted the phrase as the sum of each of its elements, starting with the word *fear*, we would instantly be off on the wrong track. Peterson states, "'Fear-of-the-Lord' is not a combination of fear + of + the + Lord. It is not the combination of four definitions. 'Fear of the Lord' is a word all its own . . . a new word in our vocabularies; it marks the way of life appropriate to our creation and salvation and blessing by God."[2] Because of the gospel, "fear-of-the-Lord" is a way of life characterized by wonder, amazement, awe, prayer, and worship.

The Need for an Update

For most of my Christian life my understanding of the fear-of-the-Lord had severely hindered my capacity to live by and enjoy the grace of God. The result was exhaustion, burnout, and depression. My perception of the fear of God was rooted in Old Testament stories such as Moses leading the Israelites on their forty-year exodus. Consider the scene when they received the Ten Commandments. God forewarned Moses that He would be descending on Mount Sinai; Moses was to set a boundary for the people not to cross. If they crossed the line to climb the mountain or even touch it they would be put to death. On the third day there was a deafening trumpet blast, fire, smoke, and thunder. The whole mountain shook. The people were so filled with terror that "everyone . . . shuddered in fear" (Exodus 19:16, MSG).

Later in Moses' story, Korah, Dathan, and Abiram

complained about Moses' leadership, so the next day the Lord opened the ground under their feet swallowing them up along with their families and all their stuff. "And that was the end of them, pitched alive into Sheol" (Numbers 16:33, MSG). Another 250 people were cremated by lightning for siding with Korah, Dathan, and Abiram against God.

Later, the Israelites complained to Moses about the lack of water. They were in a nasty mood, and they let Moses have it. So the Lord told Moses to gather everyone together in front of a rock and then speak to it; it would provide water for everyone. Moses, evidently frazzled and frustrated, instead hit the rock with his staff. As a result God told Moses that what he had given his life to, leading these people out of bondage in Egypt and into the Promised Land, was being taken away from him. He would no longer lead the people; his life dream of serving God's people was taken away.

Old Testament stories like these shaped the fear of God for me. God, it seemed, is pretty touchy, rather irritable and short-tempered. If you cross Him, His wrath is going to be unleashed, and *pow!* Stones and arrows everywhere. Earthquakes. Lightning. Demolished dreams.

I began realizing I needed to include the gospel in my understanding of the fear-of-the Lord. "There is no fear in love, but perfect love casts out fear. For *fear has to do with punishment*" (1 John 4:18; emphasis added). This is a foundational verse for understanding our freedom from fearing God, in the sense of anticipating punishment from God. The

Jerusalem Bible says that "to fear is to expect punishment" (1 John 4:18).

If punishment is gone for the believer, then so is fear.

> Love and fear are incompatible. They cannot co-exist. For the Christian, love is first an experience of the Father's love for us. That "love" is so powerful and life changing that when we know it we are forever removed from the "fear" of God.[3]

I learned I didn't have to exhaust myself trying to please an impossible-to-please God. He sees Christ's obedience as mine. My sin no longer condemns me, and I am not given the badge of sinner. I have a new name—*saint*. If I am not condemned, I will not be punished. Jesus took care of that. God is no longer my judge but my Father. What is there to fear?

Jonathan Edwards, a prominent Puritan pastor, preached a famous sermon in 1741 titled "Sinners in the Hands of an Angry God." For the listeners who had not yet placed their faith in the work of Christ, this was true. And a scary reality. As a result thousands became Christians. For believers there is a new message with good news, we are now "Saints in the Protective Embrace of a Loving Father."

Faith versus Fear

Ann Voskamp writes, "Perhaps the opposite of faith is not doubt. Perhaps the opposite of faith is fear."[4] This seems to be Jesus' response to his disciples as they were boating across the Sea of Galilee in a life-threatening storm: "Why are you so afraid?" he asks. "Have you still no faith?" (Mark 4:40).

Maybe we don't use the word *fear* to describe our relationship with God; still, we might hear ourselves using softer words, such as, *wondering*, *hesitancy*, and *timidity*. Being fearful, anxious, wary, or cautious in God's presence is a red light on the dashboard of our soul. All of these feelings are a denial of God's unending love for us. They warn us that our faith in God's unconditional love for us needs to be revisited and refreshed—updated again by the gospel. Voskamp expresses it this way: "All fear is but the notion that God's love ends."[5] It is our faith in God's gospel-love for us that allows us to approach Him *without* fear and *with* confidence and boldness. Paul, writing to his friends in Ephesus, said that "we have *boldness* and *access with confidence* through our *faith* in him" (Ephesians 3:12; emphasis added).

New Testament Fear of God

What might be an updated definition of the fear of God? Brennan Manning has written one that reflects how we should live before the Father, Son and Holy Spirit—all of whom are crazily in love with us. He defines the New Testament fear of God as "silent wonder, radical amazement, affectionate awe—at the infinite goodness of God."[6]

God does not motivate us to obey by fear of His anger, displeasure, or punishment. Philip Yancey says that "in Jesus, God found a way of relating to human beings that did not involve fear."[7] God now motivates us by His goodness. If we fear God's punishment, we obey out of self-protection; our "acts of obedience" are not acts of love but self-centered acts of self-defense. In fact, as Steve Brown asserts, "Almost anything you do with God that comes from fear is probably wrong."[8]

Failure and Fear

When I am unfaithful and feeling as though I have failed God, do I need to fear His displeasure? No. God may not be pleased with what I *did*—but He's not displeased with *me*.

When I think of biblical examples of failure, Simon Peter's repeated denials come to mind. First he denied Jesus to a young servant girl. She posed no threat to him; her role was simply to answer the door. But then, as Jesus was being interrogated by Annas, Peter was challenged again. This time he was warming his hands around a fire when some people suggested that he was one of Jesus' disciples. Peter once again vigorously denied it. When next one of the servants mentioned that he saw Peter only a few minutes earlier with Jesus, Peter vehemently repudiated the accusation. Immediately his heart sank as he realized he had just done what Jesus said he would do and what he publicly vowed he would never do: deny Jesus three times. He had promised Jesus he would never let Him down, he would never be unfaithful—even if it cost him his life. With his failure overwhelming him and sickening him to his core, "he went out and cried and cried and cried" (Matthew 26:75, MSG).

There follows two intriguing post-resurrection passages about Peter and Jesus. The first is Luke 24:34, in which two disciples, having just encountered Jesus on the road to Emmaus, reported back to the Twelve: "The Lord has risen indeed, and has appeared to Simon!" That must have been an interesting encounter—and hugely important for Peter. Using our sanctified imagination and knowing how Jesus' love reflects the Father's love, I suspect tears were streaming down Peter's cheeks as Jesus, His arm around Peter, forgave him and reaffirmed His deep and unconditional love.

But Peter needed more than forgiveness. Judas had betrayed Jesus, and in the irreversible horror of what he had done, Judas had hung himself. Peter had denied Jesus, and in the pain of his deep failure and shame, he wanted to get away and hide. So Peter announced to his fellow disciples, "I am going fishing" (John 21:3). I wonder if shame was telling him he was no longer worthy to lead, and so he decided to quietly disappear back into his career. But his disappearing didn't help. He needed to know the one he had been unfaithful to not only forgave him and still loved him, but still believed in him. Still saw good in him. Still had plans for him. Peter needed to know that he was not washed up and thrown aside.

And so Jesus initiates *another* interaction with Peter—this time in the presence of the other disciples (John 21:15-19). Brennan Manning describes the scene: "There was no sarcastic greeting like, 'Well, my fair-weather friends . . .' No vindictiveness, spite or reproach. Only words of warmth and tenderness."[9] Three times Jesus affirms Peter's worth, his future contribution, and his continued leadership: "Feed my lambs. . . . Tend my sheep. . . . Feed my sheep."

"To affirm a person," Brennan Manning writes, "is to see the good in them that they cannot see in themselves and to repeat it in spite of appearances to the contrary."[10] Jesus not only loved Peter, not only forgave Peter, but also affirmed he still believed in him. Jesus was not abandoning him.

Affirmation and Fear

Affirmation is a powerful and healing experience. It is what Peter needed after his denial of Christ. It is what I needed during my counseling intensive. I was not feeling very good about myself; actually I felt like a big mess, a huge disappointment. One day Milt, our counselor, leaned over and looked me right in the eye. "Wow, Bill," he said. "You have a really good heart." He saw something that I could not see, and as he spoke it I could feel healing taking place in me.

I think Peter needed to hear the same healing affirmation. Commentators on this passage often focus on the distinction between the two Greek words used for love in the dialogue between Jesus and Peter; *agapao* and *phileo*. Three times Jesus asks Peter if he loves Him, using *agapao* the first two times and *phileo* the third. It has been noted this change was intended to deeply challenge the depth of Peter's love, suggesting that it was only superficial. These two words are used so interchangeably in the New Testament, however, that many commentators see no significance in how they are used here. "These differences do not amount to a distinction of real theological reference; they do not specify a difference in the kind of love referred to."[11]

If that's correct, then it eliminates the idea that Jesus is gauging the sincerity of Peter's love. Jesus, after all, knows that Peter deeply loved Him. This may be why Peter bursts out in frustration, "Lord, you know everything; you know that I love you" (John 21:17). The emphasis in this encounter is not on Peter's love, but on his need for affirmation. Peter does not have to prove himself to Jesus and the other disciples. Jesus wants Peter to accept the love and approval that was always there—in spite of his recent conduct. The disciples standing within earshot hear Jesus say he is still okay with Peter and his leadership. They also hear that they will be okay with Jesus when they mess up.

We also have the privilege of being within earshot of this discussion. We fail miserably—worse than we ever dream possible. Like the psalmist in Psalm 32, our sin sickens us to the bone. In such moments our energy is gone; our motivation is gone; our hope is gone. We are sure God is disappointed, sure He wants to punish us, and so fear lurks in the shadows. Our future is washed up. There will be no crossing of the Jordan into the Promised Land for us. And soon everyone will know it.

We could not be more wrong. The Jesus that put His arm around Peter in his failures is the Jesus that puts His arm around us in ours. We hear He still loves us. He still believes in us. There remains a future and a hope for us (Jeremiah 29:11).

Risk and Fear

When we're afraid of God's punishment, we quickly determine that we're better off staying in the boat, fishing with Peter. Going back to our old life before Christ feels like our only remaining option. We don't even care if we catch no fish. We cannot serve God courageously if we fear that when we fail, God will take us off the list of those He will bless and use.

Hudson Taylor (1832–1905), a British missionary to China for fifty-one years, was the impetus for over eight hundred missionaries heading to China and founding over 125 schools. The gospel spread to every province in China, and over 18,000 Chinese became followers of Jesus. All this happened in an era when travel was slow and hazardous, and when there was no modern medicine. Every undertaking was *filled* with risk. But Taylor adamantly believed that unless there is an element of risk in our exploits for God, there is no need for faith.

In Jesus' parable of the talents (Matthew 25), a businessman is taking an extended trip and entrusts to three of his servants some of his cash assets to invest. Returning home, the first two servants return the original sum plus 100 percent interest. The third servant returns the original cash—no more, no less. And then he utters this revealing statement: "Master, I knew you to be a hard man. . . . I was afraid, and I went and hid your talent [money] in the ground" (Matthew 25:24-25). We will never risk if we fear God is a hard master. We will find ourselves digging holes in the ground, hiding ourselves and our talents. *Fear of God does not motivate; it paralyzes.* Steve Brown reminds us that "the parable was not about doing better. It was about risk."[12] When I imagine God as my hard master, I start digging holes, all designed to protect me. My most frequented hole has a sign by it "work harder" so that God won't be disappointed with my effort.

Yeah but . . .

What about Philippians 2:12, which exhorts us to "work out your own salvation with fear and trembling"? This sounds as if our Christian growth should be motivated by fear. It feels like a semi-veiled threat to work hard and be faithful—or else.

This is how I understood this verse, and I was wrong. For two reasons.

First, I discovered that if it's a subtle threat, it's also an *empty* threat. When my growth has been characterized by half-heartedness, I have not experienced a heavenly Father who makes me tremble with fear. I've discovered the opposite: a Father who woos me with His goodness and love.

Second, the person I am responding to with "fear and trembling" is not God. The person I need to be afraid of is me! Ralph Wardlaw, an eighteenth-century Scottish Presbyterian, calls the fear described in this passage as "self-distrust; it is tenderness of conscience; it is vigilance against temptation. . . . It is taking heed lest we fall."[13] Paul puts it this way, "If you think you are standing strong, be careful" (1 Corinthians

10:12, NLT). Philippians 2:12 is not a warning to mature or else; it is an exhortation for us to keep walking in humility so that we may continue to mature!

Free!

In my sin and deepest failures, I have discovered I have no reason to fear God's response to me and wonder about His commitment to me. I don't need to enter His presence with timidity and cautiousness. I am free from digging holes for self-protection.

In fact, as Donald Gray puts it, "The gospel *requires* . . . that we give up fearing the Father."[14] And so I can live appropriately in the presence of God, who by the gospel has replaced fear with wonder, amazement, and awe. I come to Him with boldness and confidence, trusting that what He tells me about His love for me is true—really true.

Martin Luther, before going to Wittenberg to study the New Testament, described himself as living "in terror of judgment." After immersing himself in the New Testament, however, he declared, "I was wrong. . . . Those who see God as angry do not see him rightly. . . . If we truly believe Christ is our savior . . . to see God in faith, is to look upon his friendly heart."[15]

Living in fear of God kills the freedom that Jesus died to give. Fourteenth-century English mystic Julian of Norwich wrote, "The greatest honor we can give Almighty God is to live gladly because of the knowledge of his love." To that I would add that we not only live gladly; we also live *freely*.

CHAPTER 8

Free to Live in Peace

THE GOOD NEWS of the gospel is incomplete if it only sets us free *from* some things. Even if what we've been set free from are horrible realities and have dreadful consequences, freedom *from* is not the whole story. Jesus set us free so that we could live in a new and different reality.

We are not set free *from* things into a blah, boring, color-less neutral zone. Jesus tells us He came so we could "have life *and* have it *abundantly*" (John 10:10; emphasis added). As the New Living Translation has it, "My purpose is to give life in all its fullness." When we have our feet firmly planted in the freedom we have been set free *for*, we find our life filled to overflowing.

The purpose of being set free *from* something is to be set free *for* something. The apostle Paul makes this clear in Galatians 5:1: "*For freedom* Christ has set us free" (emphasis added). And so we not only give thanks for a past emancipation, we celebrate living free in his kingdom now.

What we have been set free for is more healing and life-changing than we can ever imagine. The gospel releases us into freedoms that change everything about the way we live, so much so that other people actually notice—and so do we!

The Freedom of Peace

In Romans 5 the apostle Paul makes a huge transition, turning our attention from what we have been set free from, to what we have been set free *for*. "Therefore, since we have been justified by faith, we have peace with God through our Lord Jesus Christ" (Romans 5:1). We are free, Paul tells us, to experience an unfathomable and unimaginable new way of living, a peace-filled relationship with God. "Peace," Bruce Metzger suggests, "is [now] the possession of those who have been justified."[1] Not anger. Not fear. Not apprehension or wondering. Perfect peace. Permanent peace.

As Paul begins this transition, he begins with "peace with God," the most life changing transition that can ever occur in our life. We move from alienation and enmity to peace with the God of the universe!

The word "peace" in Romans 5:1 comes from the verb

eiro, meaning "to bind together that which has been separated."[2] We have been bound back to God! Picture this—you are standing with God, face to face, with His arms around you, holding you tight. Someone has tied you together with a long rope and keeps walking around you in circles, wrapping you tighter and tighter with more and more loops. Then they secure the rope with a knot.

The person circling you with the rope is Jesus. Colossians 1:20 tells us he binds us to the Father, "making peace by the blood of his cross." It's not my performance that creates this relationship—it's Jesus. He has bound us tight. There is no way we can break apart or get loose. It is impossible. In fact, as Bryan Chapell reminds us, "If God knew we were going to untie the knot of salvation, his love would require that he deny us the opportunity."[3] I love these words of the nineteenth-century hymn writer John Campbell Shairp:

> Let me no more my comfort draw
> From my frail hold of thee,
> In this alone rejoice with awe —
> Thy mighty grasp of me.[4]

This is what we have been set free for: to be bound to God. Tightly. Irreversibly.

There is another word in this verse that needs unpacking to understand this incredible freedom. We have "peace *with* God."

"With" in the original Greek is the word *pros*, meaning,

in this instance, "facing."[5] We now stand in the very presence of God, *facing* Him, guiltless, forgiven, righteous, and loved with an unconditional love. And so we can stand before Him with boldness and confidence (Ephesians 3:12). No cringing, no timidity, no wondering, no fear.

This should be the source of more than a minor adjustment in our living. All this peace is ours—now. The verb *have*, being in the Greek present tense, means that peace with God is something we have continuously in the present, right now. *Today* I have freedom to stand boldly and confidently before God—so close to Him that it is like we are bound together.

The Freedom of Friendship

For many reading these words, your family history might make the thought of being close to your father, much less bound tightly to him, a nightmare. It does not bring a feeling of freedom. Instead it brings feelings of dread and fear. It is not a place of safety but of abuse. Being bound tight to anything doesn't sound like freedom. For this reason, let's look at who Jesus has bound us to. After all, this is supposed to be good news.

First, it is important to understand that Romans 5:1 isn't dealing with "peace" as we typically think of it: a quiet, serene, or contented feeling. The peace Paul refers to here is something much more significant.

John Stott sees in this peace an act of reconciliation. "To reconcile means to restore a relationship, to renew a friendship."[6] I am reconciled with, and bound back together with God, my friend. And God is now bound together with His friend—me.

Yeah but . . .

Yeah, but do we ever hear God the Father calling us his friends? Yes and no. If I look for a direct reference, the answer is no. And yet the answer is definitely yes! Jesus tells us that we are His friends (John 15:14) and we are promised that nothing will ever be able to separate us from this loving friendship (Romans 8:37-39). Why is Jesus such a committed friend? "Why," Donald Gray asks, "does Jesus love all these losers, these failures, these no-accounts? Because the Father does."[7] Jesus is the exact representation of the Father; He only does and says what He sees the Father doing and saying (John 5:19). Jesus calls us friends because that is how He hears the Father refer to us. He treats me as a loving friend because that is how He sees the Father treating me. And why does the Father treat me as a friend? Because He sees the righteousness of Jesus in me.

Christ died for me that He might bring me to God (1 Peter 3:18). He restored my relationship, my friendship—giving me peace with God. *I am not His enemy and He is not mine.*

Free Indeed

To be bound to God the Father by the blood of Jesus is the most freeing encounter we will have this side of heaven. Freedom characterizes the Trinity: God is free; Jesus is the freest person who has ever lived; the Spirit of God blows freely like the wind (John 3:8). That's my community.

In Christ we are bound tight yet free! And "if the Son sets you free, you will be free indeed" (John 8:36)—or as it's translated in *The Message*, "You are free through and through!" That's what I need. That's what I am.

CHAPTER 9

Free to Live in Grace

THE DEFINING CHARACTERISTIC, the "governing principle,"[1] of our relationship with God is now grace. No longer is it law-keeping and its undergirding principle of performance. The governing principle of our relationship with God is not obedience or lack thereof. The governing principle is grace.

Grace: An Environment—Not a Theology

I often hear my friend Bill Thrall say, "Grace is not a theology we believe, it is an environment that we live in." Unfortunately for me, until I went through my dark night of the soul and began to get new glimpses of "the gospel of the grace of God" (Acts 20:24), grace for me was something to be studied, to be taught boldly, and to be thankful for; it was not the everyday reality of an unconditional friendship. I knew *grace* as a theological word; I needed to learn that *grace* is a *relational* word.

We might say that grace is the theology of relationship, with God and with one another. Steve Brown, in his book *A Scandalous Freedom*, asks, "Have you ever been hugged by a doctrine?" Grace as a theological concept cannot hug you, but as an environment we live in, it facilitates a relationship in which you can be unconditionally hugged.

To understand this relational experience, let's work through Romans 5:2, especially focusing on two key words: *access* and *stand*.

The Best Introduction Ever

Paul has just turned the corner from what we have been saved *from* to discuss what we have been saved *for*. Having acknowledged the peace with God which Jesus makes available to us, he now immediately emphasizes the *relationship* with God made possible through Christ.

> Through him [Christ] we have also obtained access
> by faith into this grace in which we stand, and we
> rejoice in hope of the glory of God. (Romans 5:2)

The word translated "access" here is the Greek word *prōsagogē*, which is the combination of two words: *pros*, meaning "facing"; and *agō*, meaning "to bring." Combining these words gives the meaning of being introduced into a friendly relationship.[2] A relationship of grace.

Who has introduced us into this relationship? The first two words of the verse make it unambiguously clear: it's Jesus. Nothing else gives us access—certainly not my outstanding obedience. As the apostle Peter was quick to acknowledge, "Christ . . . suffered once for sins, the righteous for the unrighteous, that he might bring us to God" (1 Peter 3:18).

Paul describes our access in a tense called "perfect" ("we have . . . obtained access"). We have no tense in English that creates the same meaning, a "completed action whose effects are felt in the present."[3] Because this tense is so infrequently used, scholars consider its use significant, conveying some deliberation and intention on the part of the author. William Mounce writes that the present perfect tense "is often used to express great theological thoughts."[4] In other words, Paul is suggesting here that our access, our introduction, to God is permanent! We don't need a new introduction after each successive sin. We never leave God's presence. We are bound tight to Him.

Standing in Grace

The second word we need to look at is *stand*. Paul writes that "we stand" in this grace. Grace is conceived of as a field into which we have been escorted and in which we are now standing, like a farmer standing in his field. But it is more than a place, it is an environment created by an unconditional relationship with our Father. This environment and relationship changes everything about how we live.

Hebrews 4:16, for example, instructs that because of Jesus we can now, with unreserved boldness and confidence, "draw near to the throne of grace." The King who sits on the throne radiates grace to everyone who comes close. Grace defines their relationship. No longer is God's throne, for the believer, a place of judgment. Could it be the more time we spend before this throne the more awestruck we are by grace?

The word *stand*, like the word *access*, is in the perfect tense, indicating ongoing effects. As John Stott puts it,

> Our relationship with God, into which justification
> has brought us, is not sporadic but continuous, not
> precarious but secure. We do not fall in and out of
> grace—no we stand in it, for that is the nature of
> grace. Nothing can separate us from God's love.[5]

Yeah but . . .

Yeah, but just a minute! If we keep talking about a relationship with God defined by this crazy description of grace, people will find a whole new way of living all right—a way filled with sin! If we stand in grace, doesn't sin cease to matter?

I think the apostle Paul heard the Pharisees using this line of reasoning. "Are we to continue to sin that grace may abound?" (Romans 6:1). Recently I was speaking at a Navigator winter retreat at a Big Ten university. I had spent two sessions describing this wild, crazy, unrestrained, no-strings-attached love. As I began the third session I realized there were some guests sitting in the back. Parents!

Immediately I started wondering what they were thinking. Was I creating an environment that would undo all their hard work of raising their sons and daughters? Would this teaching set their children free to go wild? To sin with no restraints, confident that God would love them anyway? After all, these were college kids, living away from home in an environment overflowing with temptations.

Out of insecurity as much as curiosity, I paused and asked the students if all this grace stuff made them want to sin more. Not one said, "Yes." Their response was actually the opposite: The grace of God increased their awe of God; it made them want to enjoy Him more and sin less.

When we have a new heart, freedom does not make us want to run wild and sin more. It makes us want to walk with Jesus.

The Power to Say No

Some believe grace is okay in moderate amounts, but too much grace is dangerous. They believe it loosens standards and leads people into sin, and then we have a mess to deal with. The Scriptures teach that the opposite is true. Living by the principle of law is dangerous. It is grace that *protects us* from sin. It is grace that *leads us* to godliness.

Titus 2:11-12 has been key for me in learning to trust the goodness and power of grace. "For the grace of God has appeared, bringing salvation for all people, training us to renounce ungodliness and worldly passions, and to live self-controlled, upright, and godly lives." Note that from the very beginning grace is redemptive, not destructive.[6] It brings salvation. But grace not only brings about an initial change, it serves as an ongoing force in our lives. For example, grace enables us to say no to sin. It's not our willpower, our accountability group, or a long list of rules that enables us to say no; it's grace.

Grace trains us "to renounce ungodliness," which John Calvin defines as "irreligious contempt for God."[7] Ungodliness is a state of living as though God does not exist or has no say in our life. This state of independence is, as we have seen, not the same as living in freedom. Grace says no to this type of living in favor of a close, intimate relationship with God. What God says to us matters—a lot.

Beyond this, grace trains us to "renounce . . . worldly passions." Paul is referring here to all the cravings of our flesh in which sin still dwells, which the apostle John summarizes as "the desires of the flesh and the desires of the eyes and pride of life" (1 John 2:16). On our own, we are no match for the things of the world and the desires they create in us. We find ourselves regularly saying yes to them. It is grace and only grace that enables us to say no instead.

Gerald May, in his book *Addiction and Grace*, observes that people who are addicted to habitual and repetitive sin live with mixed emotions. Part of them wants to be free from the sin and another part wants to continue the behavior. The second motivation is stronger, however, causing all resolution to stop the behavior to fail. Willpower always fails; in fact, every time a decision to stop the sinful behavior fails, the grip of the behavior tightens. "It is the very nature of addiction," he writes, "to feed on our attempts to master it."[8]

But grace, he continues, is

> the most powerful force in the universe. It can transcend repression, addiction, and every other internal or external power that seeks to oppress the freedom of the human heart. . . . Grace is our only hope for dealing with addiction, the only power that can truly vanquish its destructiveness.[9]

If grace makes believers sin, it is not really grace. Call it what it is—sensuality, license, rebellion—but don't call it grace. Don't attribute sin to the work of the gospel. Jude 1:4 teaches that living in sin is never a result of grace; rather it is the result of grace being eliminated and replaced.

> Some people have infiltrated our ranks . . . who beneath their pious skin are shameless scoundrels. Their design is to *replace the sheer grace of our God with sheer license*—which means doing away with Jesus Christ, our one and only Master. (MSG, emphasis added)

The Power to Say Yes

A second way grace is an ongoing force in our life is that it empowers us to say yes to "self-controlled, upright, and godly lives" (Titus 2:12). Notice how in this way grace supports a balanced life. Often people think grace refers only to the inner life; putting too much emphasis on grace, therefore, will distract us from an appropriate emphasis on mission. We will get out of balance.

Not so. Our mission is to reproduce mature followers of Jesus, and without grace maturity is impossible. Paul speaks of grace in holistic terms: to be "self-controlled" speaks to our inner life; to live "upright" addresses our relationships with others; to live a "godly" life refers to our relationship with God. And so without God's grace, maturity is impossible. Consequently, without grace, our mission is impossible.

In 1 Corinthians 15:9-10 Paul—one of the most mission-minded men the world has known, who ultimately gave his life for the advancement of the gospel—credits grace with *all* that is right about his life. In verse 9 he recalls his pre-Christian life as a persecutor of the church, which is chronicled in the book of Acts. If you were a follower of Christ, you did not want to see Paul coming. Paul was bent on destroying the new movement of Christ-followers. He would break into believers' homes, capture them, and throw them into prison. He was a proponent of religious cleansing by murder (Acts 8:1-3).

Paul sums this history up in 1 Corinthians 15:9 with the phrase, "I persecuted the church of God." But then he offers a huge *but* in verse 10: "But by the grace of God I am what I am." Paul was saying that *everything* that is now good about him is the result of grace.

We see great balance in Paul's new life as he communicates

grace throughout the New Testament. He longed to continually know Christ better (Philippians 3:10). He was deeply committed to Christ-like character (1 Corinthians 11:1). He had a rock-steady and unwavering commitment to the Great Commission (Philippians 1:22). Paul did not look anywhere else other than to the grace of God for balanced growth and maturity.

Eugene Peterson summarizes the result of grace's work in our lives in his translation of Titus 2:14: By grace God makes us "a people he can be proud of, energetic in goodness." Grace does not kill our motivation to live good lives— it fills us with energy to live out goodness in every area of our lives. A life of goodness is always rooted in grace. It grows no place else.

One or the Other

Okay—grace is not dangerous. But can we still mix in a few rules and laws to help believers grow? Can we have a balanced approach?

No, the Scriptures don't allow it.

Romans 6:14 was key in my recovery from burnout and depression. Paul's words—"For sin shall not be your master, because you are not under law, but under grace" (NIV)— clearly laid out the option for me: Either continue to live a law-centered life filled with lots of oughts and shoulds, and be captive to sin; or trust that I stand before the throne of grace and live in an environment of grace. Romans 6:14 declares that as believers we are no longer under law—not even a little bit. We are under grace. Does mixing in a little law help free us from sin? No, it actually does the opposite; it makes sin our master. You can't mix in only a little law. It is an all-law or an all-grace life.

When Paul learned that the believers in Galatia were being taught that they needed to keep *some* of the Old Testament law, he was incredulous. Listen to what he writes:

> I can't believe your fickleness—how easily you have
> turned traitor to him who called you by the grace
> of Christ by embracing a variant message! It is not
> a minor variation, you know; it is completely other,
> an alien message, a no-message, a lie about God. . . .
> Is it not clear to you that to go back to that old
> rule-keeping, peer-pleasing religion would be an
> abandonment of everything personal and free in
> my relationship with God? I refuse to do that, to
> repudiate God's grace. (Galatians 1:6-7; 2:21; MSG)

Paul had taught the gospel to the Galatians personally. Now they were being taught to make themselves acceptable to God by resorting to Jewish circumcision rites. Paul warns them that if they put their trust in circumcision, "Christ will be of no advantage to you. . . . I testify again to every man who accepts circumcision that he is *obliged to keep the whole law*" (Galatians 5:2-3, emphasis added). You simply can't mix law with grace. It's like practicing two religions.[10]

The Freedom of Grace

For thirty-five years I was in bondage, attempting to please people in order to find my worth. Every relationship seemed conditional, and so every decision I made was crucial to my well-being, to my future.

It was the same with God; I was always wondering if I had been good enough to please Him.

To live this way was excruciating, exhausting. Physically. Emotionally. Spiritually. The wall was waiting for me to hit it. And eventually—inevitably—I did.

And then came this life-changing glimpse of freedom— freedom that only standing in an environment of grace, surrounded by relationships of grace, can give. Jesus escorted me into an environment where performance is no longer the basis of relationship. Now I find myself standing before the throne of the King, who is also my Friend. Now I know that the unchangeable foundation of our relationship will never depend on me; it will always be the sufficiency of the life and death of Christ.

I learned this in spite of the contrary messages that so often surround me. I discovered that the gospel of grace does not put me at risk for greater sin. I am irresistibly drawn to the one who has loved me so unconditionally, and He empowers me by grace to say no to sin and yes to a virtuous life. This grace gives me really good news to share with others. I am free!

Summary of Part One

Unconditional Love and Unconditional Relationship

As I DRAW Part One to a close, let's review the individual pieces that together make up such unbelievably good news: that we are the recipients of *both* unconditional love *and* an unconditional relationship.

We began by looking at the first miracle of the gospel, that by grace God views us differently and so declares us to be righteous. In chapter 5 we discovered that this miracle frees us from performing for God's love and friendship. We dismantled the lies that our obedience causes God to love us and that our sin erodes our relationship with Him. Both His love for us and His relationship with us are unconditional.

Chapter 6 unpacked the good news of Romans 8:1, that

"there is therefore now no condemnation for those who are in Christ Jesus." Chapter 7 realized the implications of chapter 6: No condemnation means no punishment. Jesus bore all the punishment for our sin.

Building on these truths, in chapter 8 we explored how the gospel requires we give up fearing the Father. Chapters 9 and 10 then shifted our focus to what the first miracle of the gospel sets us free *for*. In Romans 5:1-2 Paul lays out the two primary fruits of our justification. At the top of the list is "peace with God." We are God's friends.

The second fruit is "this grace in which we stand." We saw that grace is our only hope. It empowers us to say no to sin and yes to godliness. It does what willpower, methods, programs, and rules cannot do. All this comes from the miracle of God's declaration that in Christ we are righteous, apart from what we do.

Putting the good news of Part One into a diagram looks like the figure on page 117.

How central should grace and peace be to our daily living? They need to be at the very core. We might be tempted to replace them at the center with the mission with which we have been entrusted: to make disciples of Jesus and shepherd them into mature faith. But when grace and peace are not at the center of our daily experience, our mission suffers; we are no longer *experiencing* the Good News we are commissioned to proclaim. We become fakes. Liars. And we know it.

Nineteen times in the New Testament, we find grace and peace front and center. Paul begins *all* thirteen of his letters

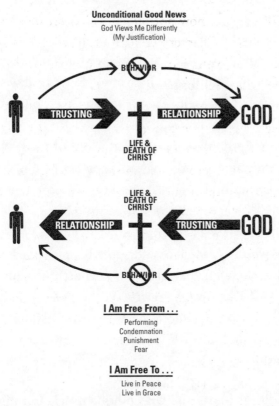

Unconditional Good News
God Views Me Differently
(My Justification)

I Am Free From . . .
Performing
Condemnation
Punishment
Fear

I Am Free To . . .
Live in Peace
Live in Grace

with this greeting, "*Grace* to you and *peace* from God our Father" (emphasis added). Through the inspiration of the Holy Spirit, Paul knew these had to be the foundational beliefs of these new and growing churches. The writer of Hebrews concludes his letter with grace and peace. Peter starts both his letters with "May grace and peace be *multiplied* to you" (emphasis mine). He wanted to see grace and peace increasing exponentially in their lives. The apostle John begins three of his four of his letters with the same greeting.

Yeah but . . .

Some wonder if this was simply a common greeting of the day, something like our "Hi, how are you?" Such a greeting is, essentially, meaningless; how often do we really *mean* for anyone to honestly tell us how they are? We wouldn't know what to do with it if they did!

The Scriptures are the inspired Word of God. Nothing is filler; nothing is meaningless. There's a reason the New Testament authors referred to grace and peace so prominently. Grace and peace would be meaningless only if the price paid for it were meaningless.

The words "May grace and peace be multiplied to you" should explode off the page, overwhelming us with a too-good-to-be-true reality, purchased at great price. They awaken us to two freedom-giving treasures God has given us: the unconditional love of God and an unconditional relationship with God.

Unconditional Love and Unconditional Relationship

Most Christians accept, at least intellectually, the first truth—that God unconditionally loves us. But few seem to accept the truth of our unconditional relationship with God. That's why for so many, the freedom Christ died for vanishes from our lives. We return to performing for God so we can meet the "standards" of a conditional relationship. The amazing *wonder* that should fill our hearts about this incredible friendship turns into *wondering* whether we have done enough. The joy and laughter of freedom is gone. "If we have to win our way back into his affection," Bryan Chapell reminds us, "we are all lost."[1]

We sinful saints are loved unconditionally and held tighter than we can imagine in an unconditional relationship. Always. No matter what. Forever. As Chapell puts it, "The struggle for God's affection is over."[2]

PART TWO

God Makes Me Different

CHAPTER 10

Miracle Two: The Transformational Good News

WHAT MORE DO we need, beyond the good news we've already considered? We need to be changed. Beyond God's work *for* us, we need a work of God *in* us. We need a new heart—a new nature from which to live. We need *regeneration*.

Just as condemnation does not make a person evil, justification does not create righteousness *in* us. Righteousness comes from what Paul calls "the washing of regeneration and renewal of the Holy Spirit" (Titus 3:5). John Murray, in his classic book *Redemption—Accomplished and Applied*, distinguishes between justification—"a judgment of God with respect to us"—and regeneration: "an act of God in us."[1] Wayne Grudem defines regeneration as "a secret act of God in which he imparts new spiritual life to us."[2]

The Old Testament prophets looked forward to this second miracle, this "secret act of God," becoming reality. God promised as much through Ezekiel:

> And I will give you a new heart with new and right
> desires, and I will put a new spirit in you. I will
> take out your stony, stubborn heart of sin and
> give you a new, obedient tender, responsive heart.
> (Ezekiel 36:26, NLT)

Why do we need to be recreated in this way? Romans 8:8 spells it out: "Those who are in the flesh cannot please God." Jesus distinguished between "that which is born of the flesh" and "that which is born of the Spirit" in His discussion with Nicodemus about the gospel; our flesh, we learn, cannot be transformed into something spiritual. How it was created is how it stays (John 3:6).

God does not transform our flesh; and neither should we—or can we. Instead He implants a new nature *in us*. And unless God does the creating, we are stuck; we cannot recreate ourselves. "God effects a change which is radical and all pervasive," John Murray tells us, "a change which is nothing less than a new creation."[3] Lewis Sperry Chafer says we have "passed through the creative hand of God a second time and . . . become a new creature."[4] It is this new creation that is the starting point and the continual source of our formation into Christlikeness.

Our new nature is foundational to our growing and

maturing in our Christian life—what theologians call our sanctification. Andrew Murray calls regeneration "the inception of being made holy . . . sanctification is the continuance."[5] Regeneration comes first, sanctification later. Without God giving us a new nature we would be unable to mature in our Christlikeness.

Being declared righteous doesn't change us. Neither does acting righteous.[6] Even acting like Jesus does not change me. Growing in Christlikeness is not the art of imitation. It is exactly the opposite. An imitation is never the real thing. For believers, growing in godliness is living authentically, out of the new us. It is living consistently with how God recreated us.

Being a New Creation—Four Key Verses

Paul returns repeatedly in his writings to the idea of new creation. Four key verses help us grasp the full significance of this reality in our lives.

> I have been crucified with Christ. It is no longer
> I who live, but Christ who lives in me. And the
> life I now live in the flesh I live by faith in the Son
> of God, who loved me and gave himself for me.
> (Galatians 2:20)

Notice everything Paul affirms in this verse. All his sins were put on Christ. What he did in the past, who he was, has been paid for. These things no longer define him; he no longer lives a Paul-centered life but a Christ centered life. Christ lives in him, and he lives by trust in the atonement.

In the midst of all of this he says another amazing thing: "I *now* live in the *flesh*" (emphasis added). Paul still had his same sin-conditioned body—the same flesh—as he did before his regeneration. In Romans 7 he says it's a flesh in which sin dwells, and this sin-steeped flesh makes him do the evil he does not want to do. It is a never-ceasing reality, a principle of life that whenever he wants to do good "evil lies close at hand," always trying to influence him (v. 21).

I "live by faith in the Son of God, who loved me and gave himself for me," but I do so in my flesh, in which sin dwells.

> Therefore, if anyone is in Christ, he is a new creation. (2 Corinthians 5:17)

It is the singular purpose of Jesus' ministry that we become new creations; without the outcome of being a new creation, Brennan Manning writes provocatively, "the Gospel is absurd and the life of Jesus is meaningless."[7] Because of what Christ has done, we are not who we used to be. We are someone different, someone new. Our essential nature is different from the person next to us that is not in Christ.

Cats cannot become dogs no matter how hard they try (even though, in my humble opinion, that would make the world a much better place). It is the same with us. We cannot recreate ourselves into someone different, no matter how hard we try, no matter how long we spend on the treadmill of self-improvement and behavior modification. Real change requires the miracle of the gospel. As Tim Keller says, "Religion tells you to go and change; the gospel changes you on the spot."[8]

This reality shouldn't have a ripple effect in our living, it should act like a tsunami. *It changes everything.*

> Put on the new self, created after the likeness of God
> in true righteousness and holiness. (Ephesians 4:24)

For me, the good news in this verse has been revolutionary. I grew up in a faithful church-going family. Dad was the church treasurer. Mom helped in summer Vacation Bible School, so we kids were there every summer. As a high-schooler I was in the youth group and went to church camp in the summer and retreats during the school year. I think most of my high school friends went to church. Yet somehow in the midst of all of this goodness, I missed the gospel.

That changed my freshman year in college, when Steve and I became friends. Near the end of our freshman year he invited me to go with him to a weekend conference sponsored by The Navigators.

On Saturday afternoon Steve and I were sitting by the lake, and he clearly and simply shared the gospel with me. It made sense; I knew I needed what the gospel offered.

The Navigators encourage Scripture memory, and one of the early verses I memorized was Jeremiah 17:9: "The heart is deceitful above all things, and desperately corrupt;

who can understand it?" (RSV). Why I selected that verse I'm not sure—maybe because it resonated with how I viewed myself. It became the template I used to define myself and to describe my heart for the next thirty-two years. It told me I had a bad heart; it was evil and could not be trusted. And so I didn't trust it. I was always suspicious and distrustful of its longings and desires. Little did I realize I was distancing and protecting myself from what Brent Curtis and John Eldredge call the "very refuge where God's presence resides."[9] It seemed a lot safer to live from a carefully scripted and crafted performance.

As Sue and I were going through our counseling intensive, one assignment was to read Brent Curtis's and John Eldredge's book, *The Sacred Romance*. It is a book about the heart, and so I was not enthused about reading it. But by page six it captured my attention. The authors talked about how so often we are trapped in our outer life living from *oughts*, rather than from the desires of our inner lives, from our hearts. That stopped me in my tracks. How could they suggest living from the desires of my heart if my heart was "deceitful above all things, and desperately corrupt?" This contradicted everything Jeremiah 17:9 had taught me. It was in direct conflict with how I lived. Then they said this:

"But can you really trust the thirst of your heart?"
the enemy whispers in my ear. "Doesn't Jeremiah,
God's own prophet, even say 'The heart is deceitful
beyond all things and beyond cure'?" And the answer

to that is "Yes." Once my heart is separated from the life of the Sacred Romance, offered to me through the atonement of Christ, and left to seek out life on its own terms.[10]

As I read these words, a glimpse of the gospel came shining through, a glimpse that would set me free. I realized Jeremiah 17:9 no longer described my heart as a believer. I had a new heart, a heart "created after the likeness of God, in true righteousness and holiness" (Ephesians 4:24), a heart that was good, that I could trust. The apostle Peter describes the new me as sharing in the divine nature. "He has promised that you will escape the decadence all around you caused by evil desires and that you will share in his divine nature" (2 Peter 1:3-4, NLT). The prophet Ezekiel prophesied that God would put a new spirit in us and give us a new obedient heart; Ephesians 4:24 demonstrates that this is now true. Michael Cusick calls this "heart transplant" "no small theological side issue."[11] Indeed. This is huge.

Because we are now described as having a new nature that is holy and righteous, as being partakers of the divine nature, we can accurately say God has not only *declared* us righteous, He has actually *implanted* his righteousness in us. He has changed us. We have a new righteous DNA from which to grow.

It was not God's intention to keep His divine qualities to Himself. He has passed us through His creative hand a second time, as believers, and made us partakers of His divine nature.

> But thanks be to God, that you who were once
> slaves of sin have become obedient from the heart.
> (Romans 6:17)

This fourth key verse tells me three important things that have changed. The first is in the phrase "you who were once," a reminder that we are not who we used to be. The gospel is transforming. It creates newness. It creates change.

Second, the phrase "once slaves of sin" assures us that we are *no longer* slaves to sin. Three verses earlier we are told how this enslavement is broken: "Sin will have no dominion over you, since you are not under law but under grace" (v. 14). As long as our strategy to deal with sin was rule-keeping, sin was our master. It is the power of God's grace that sets us free from slavery to sin.

Recognizing how sin enslaves us is critical: "For sin, seizing an opportunity through the commandment, deceived me and through it killed me" (Romans 7:11). The trick was getting us to believe that we could control our sin by keeping commandments and rules. If I can control my sin with rules, Jesus isn't necessary. Through such deception sin comes to master us.

The third way this verse informs me that I have changed is by showing me that the *source* of my obedience has changed. I "have become obedient *from the heart*" (emphasis added).

What Ezekiel prophesied would one day happen has come to pass!

These four key verses help us understand the recreated us. We live by faith, but sin still dwells in our flesh. God did not change that. Rather, He changes *us*, making us new creations with the DNA of godliness and holiness in us. We are not who we used to be. We still sin, but sin no longer needs to be our master. And we are freed from the deception that rules and commandments give us the ability to obey and please God. I now obey because *I want to* and *I can*.

Perhaps the best way to wrap all of this together is a sentence from Ann Voskamp: "I've only got one pure thing to wear and it's got Made by Jesus on the tag."[12]

CHAPTER 11

Free from Working
on Not Sinning

THERE ARE TWO gifts of the gospel without which we can become mired in our spiritual journey and increasingly bogged down in sin. Worse, we pass this faulty way of living on to others. The first gift is this: *I am free from working on not sinning.* Bill Thrall puts it this way: "When you focus on not sinning, you always sin more."[1]

The first time I heard Bill say those words, they caused a train wreck in my mind. Boxcars full of previous teaching catapulted off the tracks and lay skewed in every direction. That was a good thing; having discarded those old, rusty boxcars, I could be ready for some new ones—ones that actually work.

Rusty Boxcar #1: I Can Control My Sin

We are new creations. But we are not totally new. Nineteenth-century British preacher Charles Spurgeon wrote, "You are greatly changed. God has done wonders for you—He has put a new heart within you . . . but the inclination to evil is not dead."[2] The apostle Paul wrestled with his own inclination to evil: "I do not understand my own actions. For I do not do what I want, but I do the very thing I hate" (Romans 7:15). Why was this happening? Because of the "sin that dwells in me" (v. 17).

This old boxcar carried the assumption that we can bring sin under control by following rules, setting boundaries, disciplining ourselves to say no, and trying harder (and really meaning it). It just doesn't work. But why? Are we not trying hard enough? Is something wrong with us?

Allow me to let you in on a well-hidden secret—it doesn't work for others either! It may look like it works for some people, but those people are just really good at hiding their sin. And sin loves hiddenness—it thrives in darkness. And so it gets worse. And worse. And now there is more to hide.

Paul uses the term describing sin's compounding nature as "lawlessness leading to more lawlessness" (Romans 6:19). Sin always leads to more sin. This is why addictions cannot be controlled by effort. Wherever we draw the line, we always want more and need more, so once again we cross the line. And the "more" we need is not limited to alcohol, drugs, pornography, and sex. It includes approval, performance, being right, intimacy, being liked, lying, helping others, envy, eating, status, and an endless list of other behaviors we are enslaved to. These behaviors become our master, and we cannot serve two masters (Matthew 6:24).

The truth is you and I have no ability to deal with sin. Period. Remember Romans 7:11, "For sin, seizing an opportunity through the commandment, deceived me and through it killed me." The deception is that with enough boundaries, accountability, and effort, I can stop sinning. *The Message* expresses Paul's success with rulebooks like this: "I tried keeping rules and working my head off to please God, and it didn't work" (Galatians 2:19, MSG). It takes a miracle to deal with sin. And God has provided that miracle in Jesus Christ.

Rusty Boxcar #2: I Can Change

Okay—I can't control my sin, but can I work on changing? Sorry—no. Remember Jesus' discussion with Nicodemus in John 3:6: "That which is born of the flesh is flesh, and that which is born of the Spirit is spirit." Sin will always dwell in our flesh, regardless of how hard we work at changing it into something different. Whenever we focus on changing our flesh into something better, something more spiritual, we have undertaken the impossible. We cannot recreate ourselves.

So What Is the Answer?

What if God's intention is not to eliminate the evil and sin from our life (at least not at present), but rather to cause its agenda for us to fail? This is a microcosm of what God is doing in the grand narrative of history. It's obvious God has not yet eliminated evil from our world. We look forward to the day when God *creates* a new heaven and new earth in which evil is no more. We are not there yet, but the process has started.

How so? By the death and resurrection of Christ, which contends not just with sin in our personal lives but with all evil at work in the world, culminating with the final enemy, death. N. T. Wright, in his book *Evil and the Justice of God*, identifies evil as "the force of anti-creation, anti-life, the force which opposes and seeks to deface and destroy God's good world of space, time and matter, and above all God's image-bearing human creatures."[3] The resurrection of Jesus served a much larger purpose than our individual sin; in His resurrection, Jesus defeats the ultimate objective of evil: death.

Wright's description of evil reminds me of the contrast Jesus sets in John 10:10: "The thief comes only to steal and kill and destroy; I came that they may have life and have it abundantly." God has created in me new *life*. Every time I decide to live out of this new life, sin's purposes for me have failed. Sin still dwells in my flesh, but it is no longer killing and destroying me. It is not stealing from me. Rather I am experiencing abundant life. I am growing.

How do I grow in holiness? I live out of my new life, my new nature. I live out of who God says I now am. When I do, the goals the enemy has for me are defeated.

Does God Want Me to Change?

I remember the first time Bill asked me, "Does God want you to change?" My immediate response was, "Of course." I soon learned that this is the common response, but Bill said, "*No.*"

> God doesn't want you to change; He already has
> changed you. Now He wants you to mature out
> of the change He has already made in you.

Another boxcar replaced.

I often borrow this question as I speak on campuses and at conferences around the country. And when I share Bill's answer, many people accuse me of playing a game of semantics or splitting hairs. But the difference between *changing* and *maturing* is huge. We cannot *change into* someone different from who we are, but we *can mature into* who we *already* are.

Ephesians 4:22-24 tells us what makes up the strands of the DNA of our new creation: righteousness and holiness.

> Put off your old self, . . . [and] put on the new
> self, created after the likeness of God in true
> righteousness and holiness.

This is the DNA I mature from.

Here's an example of the difference between changing and maturing. My friend Steve Kammer sent me an interesting email as a result of implementing this paradigm for growth with college students. He asked, "Is it okay to put effort into not lying?"

I thought about it for a while and replied, "No—it's not okay to put effort into not lying. Put your effort into telling the truth."

Hair splitting? Nope—there is a big theological difference between these two options. To put our effort into not lying is trying to change our flesh into something that will be obedient and please God. This is wasted effort. To put effort into telling the truth, however, is to invest in living out of our new nature. My new nature wants to tell the truth because it's in the DNA of who I now am. We *can* grow in truth-telling. It *will* work.

Yeah but . . .

Yeah, but what about a verse like Colossians 3:5: "Put to death therefore what is earthly in you: sexual immorality, impurity, passion, evil desire, and covetousness, which is idolatry"? This sounds like Paul encouraging us to direct our efforts at not sinning.

This passage *does* instruct us to do something—and to "do it now! Do it resolutely."[4] But by itself the passage does not tell us *how* to put these things to death in us. It does not give us the method. We need the context to understand the *how*. Remember, meaning is determined by context.

In Colossians 2:20-23, Paul outlines how putting to death does *not* happen:

If with Christ you died to the elemental spirits
of the world, why, as if you were still alive in the
world, do you submit to regulations—"Do not
handle, Do not taste, Do not touch" . . . according
to human precepts and teachings? These have indeed
an appearance of wisdom in promoting self-made
religion and asceticism and severity to the body, but
they are of no value in stopping the indulgence of
the flesh.

Paul is saying the "how" doesn't reside in the "don'ts." The
don'ts don't work!

In Paul's writings, doctrine always precedes application;
truth always precedes action. If we jump to action, there is a
good chance we will get it wrong. The theology in Colossians
2:20—"With Christ you died to the elemental spirits of the
world"—is repeated in Colossians 3:3 ("For you have died")
before Paul proceeds to application in verse 5: "Put to death,
therefore . . ." Our "putting to death" of sin is tied to our
already having died *to* sin. We have died with Christ to the
mastery of sin—so let's live like it!

As we put our effort into living out of our new nature, we
are depriving sin of its power and its destructive effect on our
life. So A. T. Robertson shows us that "put to death" in Paul's
writings means "to treat as dead."[5] And then John Walvoord
encourages us to "count it to be true, and act accordingly."[6]

Paul continues on in Colossians 3:8: "But now you must
put them all away: anger, wrath, malice, slander, and obscene

talk from your mouth . . . seeing you have *put off* the old self with its practices, and have *put on* the new self" (emphasis added). The Scriptures are telling us to stop acting like you used to because it's not who you are anymore. Live out of the new you. When we do that, we rightly treat the sinful desires of the flesh as dead, and we rightly combine the theological instruction of the Scriptures with the practical application. We have combined truth with practice.

Free from What Does Not Work

Growing in Christlikeness is not opposed to effort. The gospel of grace is never opposed to *effort*—it is opposed to *earning*. But we need to put our effort in the right place: into living out of our new nature. And when we do, guess what— we sin less! But even better, "In its place you have clothed yourselves with a brand-new nature that is continually being renewed as you learn more and more about Christ, who created this new nature within you" (Colossians 3:10, NLT).

CHAPTER 12

Free to Obey

IT'S A POPULAR saying in the evangelical world: "Preach the gospel to yourself every day." Why? So we are reminded of God's incredible grace and are motivated to obey and bring glory to God. Not a bad idea. I like it. A lot. When we remind ourselves every day of the miraculous goods news of justification we find ourselves thankful beyond measure for God's grace toward us. In addition, we are overwhelmed with thankfulness for all the ways this sets us free.

We should be overwhelmed by grace. Ann Voskamp writes that giving thanks is like "unwrapping love . . . [it] multiplies the joy and makes any life large. . . . It really is a dare to name all the ways that God loves me."[1] Thankfulness is a way we stop and allow ourselves to delight in God's love for us. This places thankfulness at the very heart of our worship.

But there's a problem that thankfulness to God for our justification does not solve. It does not give us the ability or power to *obey God*. Wayne Grudem writes that justification "in itself does not change our internal nature or character at all."[2] It is merely a declaration that God makes *about* us. Without another miracle we will continue to find obedience hard and unnatural.

Thankfulness motivates but does not create ability. Motivation and ability are two different things. We need both. And God has given us both.

The Source of Obedience

I was speaking to a group of college students about the difference between motivation and ability, about Paul's acknowledgment that our flesh has "the *desire* [motivation] to do what is right, but not the *ability* to carry it out" (Romans 7:18, emphasis added). Afterward a young woman came to me with eyes moist to the point of tears. She had been taught that it was the intensity of her thankfulness that would enable her to obey. The more thankfulness, the more obedience. And so every time she struggled with obeying, she descended into a downward spiral of shame, believing there was something wrong with her and her ability to be thankful. She simply could not try hard enough.

As we talked, her tears told me that she was in the midst of being set free. She would now begin to find the power to obey in a new place: not in the strength of her motivation but in the miracle God had already worked in her.

The source of our obedience is the new heart Ezekiel wrote about: "a new heart with new and right desires . . . a new, obedient heart" (Ezekiel 36:26, NLT). This heart is given to us when we are reborn of the Spirit; without being reborn of the Spirit, all we have is our old, stony heart of flesh. We need the ability of a God-transformed heart.

Behavior change that does not come from a transformed heart is not pleasing to God. Jesus made this painfully clear when he ripped into the Pharisees for trying to change who they were by changing their behavior. It did have some surface effect because Jesus describes their outward behavior as "beautiful." They worked hard to appear "righteous" to everyone around them. They had rules and rules and more rules. But Jesus made clear that inside they were "full of hypocrisy and lawlessness" (Matthew 23:27-28).

Here is the gospel principle related to our obedience: *I do not obey so that God will do something in me; I obey because He has already done something in me.* True transformation starts on the inside, with God doing a work of recreation in us, and then it shows on the outside in our behavior. This is what Jesus warned the Pharisee, "First clean the inside of the cup and the plate, that the outside may also be clean" (v. 26).

The apostle John wrote of the source of our obedience:

People conceived and brought into life by God don't make a practice of sin. How could they? God's seed

is deep within them, making them who they are. It's
not in the nature of the God-begotten to practice
and parade sin. (1 John 3:9, MSG)

John uses the metaphor of "seed" to refer to our new divine
nature; Paul says this seed "gives . . . both the desire and
power to do God's will" (Philippians 2:13, NLT). Craig S.
Keener in his commentary writes, "A child was believed to
inherit his or her father's nature through the seed, hence John
is able to use this image to make his point: those who are
born from God through conversion reflect his character now
in them . . ."[3] The DNA of his character is now in us.

Peter also writes about this second miracle of the gospel
that implants the ability to obey: "His divine power gives us
everything we need for living a godly life. . . . He has promised that you will escape the decadence all around you caused
by evil desires and that you will share in his divine nature"
(2 Peter 1:3-4, NLT; emphasis added).

Kenneth Samuel Wuest writes in his *Word Studies from
the Greek New Testament*, "This divine nature implanted in
the inner being of the believing sinner, becomes the source
of his new life and actions." In 1 Peter 1:23, Peter further
connects our behavior with our new nature by encouraging
us to "love one another earnestly from a pure heart, *since* you
have been born again" (1 Peter 1:22-23, emphasis added).
Our love now comes from a pure heart. And why is our
heart pure? Because we have been born again. We have been
changed by God.

So—where does the ability to obey come from? It comes from being a new creation in Christ. From the new us. *Obedience is living consistently with who we now are.* It is never trying to become someone different.

New Ability, New Understanding, and New Power!

Ezekiel prophesied that God would give us "a new heart . . . *and* a new spirit" (Ezekiel 36:26, emphasis added). Jesus referred to this new indwelling of the Spirit in John 14:16-17: "I will ask the Father, and he will give you another Helper, to be with you forever, even the Spirit of truth. . . . You know him, for he dwells with you and *will be in you*" (emphasis added). Along with our new nature comes the presence of the Holy Spirit in us! John Calvin describes this unbelievable resource as "the Master or Teacher of truth,"[4] because as Jesus says, "When the Spirit of truth comes, he will guide you into all the truth" (John 16:13). In the Holy Spirit we now have a personal guide leading us and teaching us how to live out of our new DNA of righteousness and holiness. Godly living is not guess work; the Holy Spirit guides us, saying, "This is the way, walk in it" (Isaiah 30:21).

The Spirit doesn't simply guide us; He also empowers us. Paul prayed for the church in Ephesus to be "strengthened with power *through his Spirit* in your inner being" (Ephesians 3:16, emphasis added). The power the Spirit provides to walk in obedience is beyond anything we can grasp with our minds. This power is vast—reaching far beyond "all that we ask or think, according to the power at work within us" (v. 20).

A few years ago Sue and I toured the Glen Canyon Dam, which holds back the massive, 180-mile-long Lake Powell in the American Southwest. We took the elevator down seven hundred feet into the heart of the enormous dam. Deep in the bowels of the dam are eight monstrous turbines, turning equally large generators, capable of producing gobs of electricity. When we were there, the lake was at a historically low level, and not all the turbines and generators were in use. Without water falling hundreds of feet through the penstocks to turn the turbines, no electricity was being produced. The ability was there, but without the water it lacked power.

I often wonder if I'm like those generators. My new nature gives me a new ability, but I need power to go with it. The Holy Spirit not only teaches me and guides me in the way I should go, He gives me the power to do it.

What about Putting in Effort to Obey?

So what is the place of our effort? What about things like discipline, hard work, and self-control? Two quick truths. First, grace is never opposed to effort—it is opposed to *earning*. Second, self-control, discipline, and the like are not the *cause* of what God does in us, they are the fruit of what God *has done* in us.

Immediately after talking about having "become partakers of the divine nature" (2 Peter 1:4), the apostle Peter writes at length about effort. "For this very reason, *make every effort* to supplement your faith with virtue, and virtue with knowledge, and knowledge with self-control, and . . .

brotherly affection with love" (v. 5, emphasis added). The length of this list (and I left a lot out) is not the important point; what is key is the *reason* we are to make this effort: We have become partakers of a new divine nature. Notice what comes first . . . God's work in us. Then we make every effort, empowered by the Spirit in us, to live out of this new life.

There is one more important observation about effort here. As Peter comes to the end of the list, he characterizes these things as "*qualities*" (v. 8, emphasis added). The Scriptures make an important distinction between *qualities* and *behaviors*. We are to put our effort not into behaviors but into living out the qualities of the new us.

Love, for example, is not a behavior. It is a strand of the DNA of godliness that God has implanted in us. Love behaves uniquely in every different situation. Sitting with a friend in the surgical waiting room while his wife is having cancer removed, or something as mundane as emptying the dishwasher for Sue, are behaviors rooted in the quality of love, which is part of the new nature God has given me.

When Peter says we are to put effort into adding all these qualities together, he is not giving us a list of what we are to do; if the Scriptures listed behaviors that I am to put effort into, the list would be endless. Rather, Peter is telling us to live out of all of who we are.

Yeah but . . .

One passage I am asked about almost more than any other is Colossians 3:12-14, where we are told to "put on . . .

compassionate hearts, kindness, humility, meekness, and patience . . . and above all these put on love." I misunderstood and misapplied this passage for years, and it kept me chained to the treadmill of always needing to try harder. I used to read this and say to myself, *Yikes, this is everything I am not . . . I have a lot of work to do.* I envisioned myself putting on all these qualities like clothes, covering up the real me and hoping the qualities would change me from the outside in. If I could just act differently long enough, I might have a chance. After all, I knew Ralph Waldo Emerson's advice: "Sow an act, reap a habit; sow a habit and reap a character."

With due respect to Ralph, this passage means exactly the opposite. Note how this passage describes us: "God's chosen ones, holy and beloved" (3:12). I already *am* something I could never make myself—a new creation! I am to let this new creation come to the surface, like a beautiful new wardrobe, so people can see it. I discard and *put off* those things that are inconsistent with who I am and I *put on* those things that are now true of me. I am not trying to put on something I am not; I am trying to live in accordance with who I am. This requires a miracle of God in me, and in the gospel it has become reality!

Obedience versus Compliance

Obedience is no longer rooted in what we are told or what we know we should do. Obedience is now rooted in *trust*— trust that who God says we are is true and so we act accordingly. This makes obedience a relational word, something that happens in an environment of trust. *Obedience is the evidence of my trust*, and Hebrews 11:6 tells us that it is our faith, our trust, that pleases God.

It is not our obedience that pleases God; it is the relationship of trust that we have with Him that results in our obedience. In fact, doing what is right without a relationship is not gospel obedience.

We often do things not because we trust someone but because we fear their power and their ability to bring consequences. This is called compliance. When my sons would do things simply because of the consequences they would experience if they didn't, it never pleased me. It discouraged me. They did not trust that my intentions and desires for them were good. My relationship with them in those moments was simply one of power.

There is no freedom in compliance. You are reduced to being the slave of a more powerful task master. But in obedience, rooted in a relationship of trust, we are free. We are free from trying to change because God has already changed us. We are free from having to work on not sinning and can now focus on *living* from a new and obedient heart. We are free to live out of an ability we never had before . . . out of a supernatural power beyond ourselves. Our obedience as believers is no longer the result of impending consequences; it finds its home in a deep trust of our Father, who is always good, always loving. He knows what is best, and a relationship of trusting obedience is a safe place for us.

CHAPTER 13

Free to Love

I WAS A chemistry major. I took lots of math and physics. I am an ISTJ on the Myers-Briggs Type Indicator (MBTI), a profile described as rational, logical, and methodical. An ISTJ is not naturally in tune with their feelings or the feelings of others; please don't ask me how I feel about something—or if you do, give me a list of choices I can pick from.

ISTJs are not known for their emotional warmth. They care deeply about people but it is tough and tiring to express. Add to my ISTJ personality the lies that formed me into a people pleaser, and maybe you can understand why I have had difficulty both receiving and giving love.

I have a hunch that a lot of people—my fellow ISTJs, "legalistic" and "moralistic" people, as well as a host of wounded performers—are ready to skip this chapter. Love makes the Christian life way too touchy-feely—too soft, too undisciplined, too unprincipled, and way too unpredictable. It makes us people-pleasers feel unprotected.

The Bible is full of principles and guidelines about right and wrong that love shouldn't overrule, we think. If we focus our faith on love alone, we fear we will lose our footing in the Scriptures and just be led by our feelings. We will use love as an excuse to ignore biblical commands. Horrors! People like this are dangerous.

How do I know some of you are reacting like this? Because I did and God tells me I am not unique. I meet reminders of me all the time. Grappling with the Scriptures I am going to share has been key to loosening the chains of shame and performance. Even though at times I can still hear those old chains rattling, I now see things in God's Word I never saw before. Dots are being connected between what I formerly suspected were disjointed and irritating inconsistencies. I see a thread and a message I never saw before: God's message to us, and His desire for us. There is nothing that is safer.

Love Is the *Expression* of Faith

Our son David and his fiancée Hannah asked me to be a part of their wedding ceremony by giving the scriptural meditation and charge to them as a couple. They also "suggested" the passage of Scripture they wanted me to emphasize,

Galatians 5:6: "For in Christ Jesus neither circumcision nor uncircumcision counts for anything, but only faith working through love." I trust that what I said to Dave and Hannah was helpful and meaningful. (It looks like it has been!) For me it was a time of grappling with a verse I would rather have skipped over. Dave and Hannah could not have picked a better verse—for me.

Paul begins the verse with three life-altering words: "in Christ Jesus." Nothing in all of human history is more transformative. Christ Jesus is always a turning point.

For the Jews who trusted Christ in the first century, this verse transformed a whole way of living, of relating to God, and thousands of years of religious tradition. Relentless rule keeping and adherence to the law was being voided, declared useless. Jesus had established a new way of relating to God "apart from the law . . . through faith in Jesus Christ" (Romans 3:21-22).

Paul continues in his encouragement to the Galatians: "the only thing that counts," he tells them, "is *faith expressing itself in love*" (NIV, emphasis added). The word *only* feels like a bad news word, because it's exclusive; I can't add anything to faith, and whatever I might add doesn't count.

I enjoy getting credit for my effort. I like rewards. But this *only* is really good news: anything I might add wouldn't do me any good, so I am set free from insanely trying to please God by making myself acceptable to him. Faith that expresses itself in love is the *only* thing that counts!

This is strong language. God moves love—and love

only—to the front and center as the way my faith is displayed to others. Why can't I have morality, conservatism, discipline, or something else as the primary evidence of my faith? How about not wearing jeans to church? Short hair? No tattoos?

God tells me no, there is nothing else that counts. It is love and love only. Commentator Ernest de Witt Burton writes, "There is no more important sentence in the whole epistle, if indeed, in any of Paul's epistles."[1] It can't be downplayed.

John 13:35 records this teaching of Jesus: "By this all people will know that you are my disciples, if you have love for one another." How do we prove to the world that we are followers of Jesus with a transformed heart? By our love for one another.

My friend Bill loves to misquote this verse: "People will know you are my disciples because you sin less than they do." But in reality, he adds, "my unbelieving neighbors aren't impressed with how little I sin. They are impressed with how well I love them." John Chrysostom (344–407 AD) agrees: "Miracles do not attract unbelievers as much as the way you live your life. And nothing brings about a proper life as much as love."[2]

When I was helping launch the Navigator ministry at the University of Kentucky, I was confronted by a staff member: "Bill, the students you are meeting with don't feel like you love them." Ouch! This hurt. But he was right. I had invested my energies in studying theology, church history, and biblical

Greek; I had neglected what should have been the primary expression of my faith: love.

Moreover, because I was still trapped in people pleasing, any expression of love I did attempt with students always contained mixed motives. I was loving them for some other purpose. People can sense our mixed motives no matter how well we think they are hidden. They know that what we give is always outweighed by what we take.

Love Is the *Evidence* of Faith

Our ability to live in the freedom of loving others is not just for their good, so they will know we are transformed followers and lovers of Jesus; it is for *our* good, so *we* will know God has done a miracle in us.

First John 3:18-19 encourages us to "not love in word or talk but in deed and in truth. By this we shall know that we are of the truth." Love is not just the *expression* of my faith to *others*; it is the *evidence* of my faith to *me*. John Calvin put it this way: "If we, in truth, love our neighbors, we have an evidence that we are born of God."[3]

Gregory of Nyssa, an early church theologian living in the 300s, asserts that if "God is love" (1 John 4:8), and if His nature and likeness have been "fashioned" and implanted in us, then the ability to love will be reflected in us for all to see—including ourselves. Conversely, "if love is absent, the whole stamp of the likeness is transformed."[4] In other words, if we say we are new creations with a new heart created after the likeness of God, but we don't express the loving character of God, then by our behavior we project a distorted and corrupted image of God.

How do I know I belong to the truth and that God has done a new work in me? I see myself loving people with authentic actions. This is part of my new identity: It is who I am. As Mark Bates preached to his congregation, "You are not what you do; you do who you are."[5]

Why Is Love a "New Commandment?"

In John 13:34, Jesus says, "A new commandment I give to you, that you love one another: just as I have loved you, you also are to love one another." Why is this a "new" command? After all, Leviticus 19:18 gave a very similar command: "You shall love your neighbor as yourself." And when the Pharisees asked Jesus what was the greatest commandment in the law, Jesus answered that, after loving God, loving your neighbor is greater than all the rest. Even John writes later that this is "no new commandment, but an old commandment that you had from the beginning" (1 John 2:7).

So why does Jesus call this commandment "new"? There are two reasons that are inseparably bound together.

First, there is a shift in the command, from loving others "as yourself" to loving one another "as I have loved you." That is a huge change, and impossible for us to make ourselves—except for the second reason: we now have a new nature and the Spirit of Christ in us. We can love one another as Jesus has loved us because of what God has done in us. This command is new because for the first time we can do it.

Free!

What sets us free to love others as Jesus loves us? The first miracle of the gospel, our justification, deeply *motivates* us to love. But it is this second miracle of God, actually changing us and planting his Spirit in us, that gives us the *ability* to do what we are so motivated to do. With both in place, we are set free to love.

CHAPTER 14

Free to Bear Good Fruit

I OWE THIS short chapter to my friend Del Tackett. Del and I have enjoyed dinner together once a month for ten years. One evening as we were indulging on grilled bratwurst, I was sharing the chapter outlines for the book. Del stopped me and said I was missing a foundational chapter—our new nature sets us free to bear good fruit. He was right. Bearing fruit overlaps with being free to obey and free to love, but it is both bigger and unique. In Matthew 7:17-18 Jesus discusses the nature of fruit:

> So, every healthy tree bears good fruit, but the
> diseased tree bears bad fruit. A healthy tree cannot
> bear bad fruit, nor can a diseased tree bear good fruit.

We don't attach fruit to a random tree to make it a fruit tree. It's the other way around—the tree creates the fruit. Consequently, the quality of the fruit is contingent on the quality of the tree; whether the fruit is good or bad depends on the health of the tree. Fruit always reflects the essence or the nature of the tree. And so Jesus says later in Matthew,

> The tree is known by its fruit. . . . The good person out of his good treasure brings forth good, and the evil person out of his evil treasure brings forth evil. (12:33,35)

In an earlier chapter we saw Jesus tearing into the Pharisees for their hypocrisy of attaching good-looking fruit to bad trees. They appeared righteous on the outside but inside they were anything but. Jesus corrected the backward order they were going about things, "First clean the inside . . . then the outside also will be clean" (Matthew 23:26). Fruit that pleases God comes from a transformed inner man . . . from a good tree. The Pharisees were banking their eternity on behavior modification. Behavior modification is not the gospel.

Our Fruit Reflects Our New DNA

Where does good fruit come from in our lives? John Calvin attributes it to God's work of regeneration in us, "for this end—that by newness of life we may bring forth . . . holiness and righteousness."[1] Ephesians 4:24 describes our regenerated new nature as "created after the likeness of God in true righteousness and holiness." How do we bear fruit that is pleasing to God? We do it by living out of our new nature.

Moreover, Galatians 5:22 ties the same fruit to the work of the Spirit in us. Without the Spirit in us, there would be no fruit. It is these two contributing factors—our new nature and the indwelling of the Spirit—working together in us to bear fruit that pleases God.

Legalism tacks on behavior. God produces fruit. Complying with the law and bearing fruit are two fundamentally different things, as Galatians 5:22-23 makes clear: "The fruit of the Spirit is love, joy, peace, patience, kindness, goodness, faithfulness, gentleness, self-control; *against such things there is no law*" (emphasis added). We can make laws and standards regarding behavior—speeding, murder, stealing, abuse, jaywalking, and on and on. Then we can hold one another accountable for behavior; this is what law does. But we cannot make laws that deal with the inner qualities from which our behavior comes.

This is easiest to illustrate in the negative. You can make a law against speeding, but you cannot make a law that goes inside me and deals with the impatience that leads me to speed. You can outlaw murder or theft, but you can't make a law that deals with the hatred or greed inside me. So when the Scriptures say, "Against such things there is no law," we understand that "such things" are qualities and not behaviors. The fruit of the Spirit represents deep inner qualities God has planted in us; they define who we are.

Free!

God making me different has set me free from legalism, moralism and performance, in which I tried to become someone different from who I was on the outside. On my own, that was all I could do—work from the outside in. Thankfully God worked a miracle in me, starting on the inside, remaking the real me into someone really good! I am not a Jeremiah 17:9 mess. I am a good tree that has the motivation, ability, and power to bear good fruit.

Summary of Part Two

A New Ability and New Power

In Part Two we looked at a second miracle of the gospel—that God has made us different. He planted *in* us His divine nature. We have not only been declared righteous, His righteousness has been implanted in us. Jesus described it as being "born again" (John 3:3). John wrote of this new creation as having its source "not of blood nor of the will of the flesh nor of the will of man, but of God" (John 1:13). As Paul said, "When you were dead . . . God made you alive with Christ" (Colossians 2:13, NIV).

This new heart of ours actually *wants* to obey. Sinclair Ferguson writes, "We receive new dispositions. . . . We may not yet be perfect, but we *are* different."[1] Moreover, not only do we *want* to obey, we *can* obey, because we have a new influence and power in us: the Holy Spirit.

This miracle of God changing us by a new birth frees us from our fruitless attempts of trying to become righteous. We can now focus our effort on something that will work: living out of the righteousness He has implanted in us. We can obey. We can love. We can bear fruit.

Here is what this looks like when we put the freedoms of Parts One and Two together:

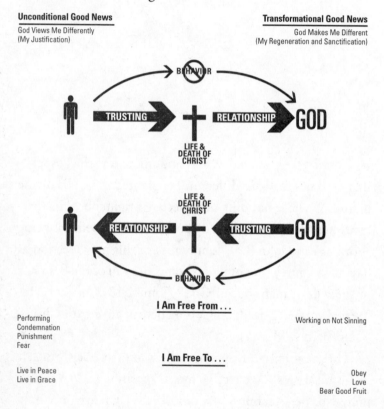

Unconditional Good News
God Views Me Differently
(My Justification)

Transformational Good News
God Makes Me Different
(My Regeneration and Sanctification)

BEHAVIOR
TRUSTING   RELATIONSHIP   GOD
LIFE & DEATH OF CHRIST

LIFE & DEATH OF CHRIST
RELATIONSHIP   TRUSTING   GOD
BEHAVIOR

I Am Free From . . .

Performing
Condemnation
Punishment
Fear

Working on Not Sinning

I Am Free To . . .

Live in Peace
Live in Grace

Obey
Love
Bear Good Fruit

PART THREE

God Relates to Me Differently

CHAPTER 15

Miracle Three: The Relational Good News

AFTER IMMERSING OURSELVES in the wonders of our justification (Part One) and regeneration (Part Two) it's hard to believe there is still more good news. But there is a third miracle—our adoption as children of God.

For God to be our Father, and for us to be His children, is the ultimate purpose of God. J. I. Packer calls it "the climax of the Bible."[1]

> What is a Christian? . . . The richest answer I know
> is that a Christian is one who has God as Father.[2]

With the Reformation's emphasis on justification by faith and our continuing need to emphasize it, the miracle of our adoption can be lost in the shadows. But, as John Murray puts it, "Adoption is an act of God's grace distinct from and additional to the other acts of grace . . . a distinct act carrying with it its own particular privileges."[3] They are the richest privileges we have, and it is devastating to us when we lose our grip on them.

God's Ultimate Purpose

Our adoption as children of God is not a postscript to God's plan. It's His ultimate purpose, a purpose that reaches into eternity past. "Before the foundation of the world . . . he predestined us for adoption as sons through Jesus Christ" (Ephesians 1:4-5). Our adoption, in the words of Dan Culver, "was in God's triune mind and heart before the first tick of human history's clock."[4]

God's intention goes beyond simply justifying us, beyond creating in us a new nature. It has always been God's intent to bring us "into the warmth, love, and gladness of his own family."[5] If God justified us without adopting us, we would stand guiltless before Him but never experience an intimate relationship with Him. If God gave us new life without adopting us, we would be receptive to His Word, but we'd be alone, with our deepest longings for relationship unmet.

Adoption is unique—it's about relationship; how we relate to God as our Father, how He relates to us as His children, and how we relate to one another as the family of God.

God Is My Father

The privileges of our adoption are beyond comprehension—and beyond the scope of this book. But there is *one* privilege God wants us to know well—the privilege of accessing God as our Father.

Jesus teaches his disciples to pray beginning with "Our Father" (Matthew 6:9). This was scandalous to the Jews in his day and invited death by stoning. We never see the Jews addressing God as "Father" in the Old Testament. By beginning his prayer in this way, Jesus is telling us *we must change the way we think about God.*

Jesus introduces an unimaginable intimacy with God by calling God "Abba" (Mark 14:36). *Abba* was an Aramaic word used by both children and adults to express intimacy and affection for parents.[6] Today we might use the term *dad* or *daddy*. This changes everything about how we relate to God. As believers, we are no longer subject to a distant, uninvolved task master—God is our Father, *and* our friend.

We Are His Children

If God is our Father, then we are His children. Galatians 3:26 declares, "For in Christ Jesus you are all sons of God." And so, as Packer puts it, "The gift of sonship to God becomes ours not through being born, but through being born again."[7] Sonship is a gift of grace. Sinclair Ferguson calls it "the apex of creation and the goal of redemption. . . . It is the goal of Christ's coming."[8] Packer says that "*the entire Christian life has to be understood in terms of it. Sonship must be the* controlling thought—the normative category, if you like—at every point."⁹

Why did Paul never speak of women becoming daughters of God? Was he demeaning women? He was actually doing the opposite. In New Testament times sons inherited their father's wealth. Daughters inherited nothing. By including women in the category of sons, Paul was communicating they were full recipients of all the riches of the kingdom of God. "In Christ Jesus *you are all sons of God*. . . . There is *no male and female*, for you are all one in Christ Jesus . . . heirs according to promise" (Galatians 3:26-29, emphasis added).

Jesus Is Our Brother

If we are sons of God, then Jesus is our elder brother (Romans 8:29). And not only is Jesus our brother; we also are His. Hebrews 2:11 tells us Jesus is not ashamed to call us His brothers. He is proud of us—of me, of you. God is not ashamed of us! And this is true every day.

We Are a Family

If we are sons of God and Jesus is our elder brother, then we believers are a family—brothers and sisters to each other. We are siblings. The Greek word for brother, *adelphos*, consists of two words, *a* meaning "from," and *dephus* meaning "womb."¹⁰ And so *adelphos* refers to those who come from the same womb. We all as believers share God's last name. And because we belong to the household of God (Ephesians 2:19), we belong to each other.

As brothers and sisters in the same family, "we cannot be solitary, isolationist, or individualistic."[11] The gospel never moves us toward independence; rather it moves us in love toward each other. The ruling principle in God's family is love.

Our adoption capstones our new gospel identity. In justification, God declares that our identity is not based on our performance; we have an identity gifted to us by the performance of Jesus. The miracle of regeneration tells us we are not who we used to be. We have a new heart. Our adoption completes our new identity; we are now beloved children of God. That's who we are. John seems to shout this when he writes, "How great is the love the Father has lavished on us that we should be called the children of God! *And that is what we are!*" (1 John 3:1, NIV; emphasis added).

A Completed Love

God loves us completely, but we most fully *experience* the fullness of His love in our adoption. To not live fully in our identity as His beloved child is to only partially experience God. It is to live relationally incomplete. Unfulfilled. Lonely.

I wonder if our adoption isn't the deepest longing of God for us. Why? Because in being His children we discover who we were designed to be; we discover the lavishness of His love. There is nothing better.

CHAPTER 16

Free from Shame

FREEDOM FROM SHAME is one of the most transforming gifts of the gospel—and perhaps the least embraced. Each miracle of the gospel frees us from our shame in a unique way. Our adoption deals shame its final blow.

My shame repeatedly lied to me. It communicated I didn't have much worth, that I had an inherit stupidity that needed to be hidden. Your shame might tell you different lies. But when shame speaks, life is neither fun nor free.

Without understanding and trusting God's work *for* us and *in* us, we find no solution to our shame. None! Every other way out is a dead end, and the shame remains and even grows. But there is a solution. There really is.

What Is Shame?

Shame is not hard to understand—we all have it. It's just hard to admit. Ed Welch calls shame "the heart disease of this and every era."[1]

The easiest way to understand shame is to contrast it with guilt. Guilt tells me I have *done* something wrong. Shame tells me there is something wrong *with* me. I not only feel it, I also believe it. To me, it is who I am.

Both guilt and shame are the result of sin. Guilt, however, is a gift from God; it is designed to lead us to repentance and back to the path of life (Psalm 16:11). Shame, by contrast, is a lie. It contradicts what God says is true about us as believers, telling us we don't have worth. Shame has an abundance of untruths it is fond of telling us:

I'm dirty.

I'm broken.

I'm stupid.

I'm unlovable.

I'm defective.

I'm a mistake.

I'm not good enough.

I'm evil.

I'm unfixable.

I don't count.

I don't deserve anything good.

I don't deserve to live.

Shame shouts that there is something desperately wrong with us. And there is—apart from Christ. But in Christ we are freed from these toxic pronouncements.

The Origin of Shame

Shame showed up in the Garden of Eden immediately after Adam and Eve sinned (Genesis 3). Their "eyes were opened," and suddenly there was something that they did not want the other to see, did not want God to see, nor did they want to see it themselves. So they hid—from each other, from God, from themselves.

Shame and hiding are inseparable. Ed Welch writes that while I am declared guilty in the privacy of a courtroom, my shame is visible in community, and so it demands hiding. As Welch says, "The horror of shame is the isolation."[2]

Adam and Eve exerted creative effort in using fig leaves to hide: they didn't just rip leaves off a tree and hold them in strategic locations, they pioneered the concept of sewing. They designed personally tailored loincloths; their hiding took creativity, time, effort. Unfortunately (or perhaps fortunately), it didn't work. How do we now? First, Adam and Eve hid from God (3:8). Adam admits that despite his creative solution to his shame, he is still afraid (v. 10). And they resort to blaming: Adam blames Eve, and Eve blames the serpent (vv. 12-13). Fear, hiding, and blaming are all evidence of unresolved shame.

And there are more—denial, anger, performance, lying, exaggerating, perfectionism, struggles with body image, compulsive behaviors, and drivenness. All of these are just *symptoms*. The *issue* is our shame.

God intervened in Adam and Eve's failed attempts to deal with their shame. He made them garments of skin— garments that required a sacrifice of blood (3:20). A redemptive act is the only way shame can be dealt with, that is what we have in Christ. We can never work our way out of our shame. Never. Thanks to God, we don't have to.

Journeying from Shame to Wholeness

Everyone has a life story filled with shame. Since Adam and Eve fell in the Garden, there is no escaping from it. But there is a more personal cause: Our individual and unique shame results from both our sin and the sin of others against us.

Everyone sins. Everyone is sinned against. And so the issue is never whether we have shame, but rather how will we deal with it.

Paul Eppinger, a student at Fort Lewis College in Durango, Colorado, had an intense struggle with shame. He wrote this to his dad:

> This is embarrassing, sitting in the student union
> with tears streaming down my face. It makes me
> so sad to see people around me being happy all the
> time, living lives with purpose and direction and
> clarity. *I feel like they swept the floors of the people
> factory and pasted the leftovers together to make me*;

introducing the human collage . . . I'm very tired of hiding. I wish I were a rock.[3]

After writing these words, Paul ended his journey of dealing with his shame by committing suicide. Mingled in with all his quiet and restless thoughts was the haunting message that he was an empty collection of leftovers. Rubbish on the floor.

Reading Paul's thoughts I find memories of a place I used to live. There are feelings of visiting an old home. Sometimes there is a tug to return—I hear the whisper of the lies and the rattle of old chains. But by the grace of God I shall not return. I have discovered a way to freedom and wholeness that is not a dead end. This way works. It is transforming. It gives life. The journey from shame to wholeness is a journey of trusting the gospel. It worked for me and it will work for all the Pauls who live so quietly around us.

A Threefold Gospel Solution

Our shame is the result of identifying ourselves with sin—our own sins and other's sins against us. Therefore, as Adam and Eve discovered and as we learn in our futile attempts to cure our shame, our shame necessitates a redemptive solution. It requires the gospel. Jesus did not just take my guilt to the cross; he took my shame as well.

Shame has three enslaving bonds, each dealt with by one of the three miracles of the gospel.

First, to be free from my shame I need a *new identity*. My

sinful behavior, the unresolved issues of others, and their sinful actions against me all create in me an identity that I want to hide. I am dirty. Broken. Unlovable. Worthless. A bunch of left-over pieces. Sin has given me an identity, it has *condemned* me. The miracle of *justification* gives me an identity that is no longer linked to my behavior or my environment. My identity is now based on the behavior of Jesus. I'm not worthless. I am not stupid. I am a saint.

How about you—what identities are you set free from?

God may view me as a saint, but nothing in my lived reality has actually changed. My shame still has a grip on me, telling me I am as bad as ever. To be free from my shame I also need a *new reality*. The gospel miracle of *regeneration* eradicates shame's lies. I am a new creation. Now! I have a new nature patterned after the likeness of God in righteousness and holiness. I have a new heart—not the repulsive heart Jeremiah 17:9 describes. And I have it now. I have a new reality to live into.

Again, how about you? Is this grip of shame broken because you are embracing your new reality as a believer?

Shame engenders fear. If you discover who my shame tells me I am, you will reject me. Somehow I will be more alone than I am now. And so I continue to hide, and I strengthen my protective shield. The third gospel miracle—the miracle of adoption—breaks this last tight grasp of shame. My adoption inserts me into a family where I will never be rejected or excluded. I am always included. Always held tight. I always belong. I am in a family where I am always honored and where nothing will ever separate me from my Father's love (Romans 8:38-39). And my elder brother, Jesus, will always love me and be proud of me (Romans 8:35). I'm in a family that when I stop sewing fig leaves and pretending all is well, my siblings won't distance themselves from me; they will come closer. Safely bound to this family, my hiding is history.

How about you? Are you still in hiding or in disguise, or are you out in the free open spaces of the family of God surrounded by kin who love you just as you are? As a believer, you no longer call the dark your home. You have a new home that is completely safe.

Now, this requires action on your part. All of us need to find some family members who allow us to take off our masks and who will love us as we are. How do we know when we have found someone like this? When practicing humility and telling the truth about what we are really like draws them closer and deepens their commitment to us. We feel their arm around our shoulder and they hold us tight. When we become a part of a family like that, we are home.

Free!

To be set free from our shame is to be released to experience what God desired for us from before the foundation of the world. When we are living out of our new identity, allowing our new nature to shape us, and living as sons and daughters of a loving Father, we are exactly what God wants us to be—*free!*

CHAPTER 17

Free to Be Loved

OUR NEW NATURE gives us the ability and power to *give* love. Our adoption capstones our freedom to *receive* love. For many of us that is really hard. It makes us feel very uncomfortable. And without a miracle of the gospel it is impossible.

Receiving the Love of God
In my gospel journey, adoption affirms how completely I can trust God. He is not my enemy. He is not my judge. He is my Father. My Abba. He is always for me —always wants my best. I can trust Him.

And because I can unreservedly trust Him, I can unreservedly obey Him, knowing it will always be good for me.

When I do, I find myself abiding in His love, experiencing the extravagant love He floods his children with. "How great is the love the Father has lavished on us, that we should be called the children of God" (1 John 3:1, NIV).

Receiving the Love of Others

God made me to be loved—by Him and also by others. But for me to be loved by others, God has to perform a couple of miracles. First, He needs to give *others* a new nature so they can actually love me—just as He gave me a new nature, so I am free to love them. Second, God must place me in a family with these people, where the commitment is to love one another regardless of the messy truth they humbly reveal about themselves. And so He adopts me.

There remains only one catch: I have to *let* this family love me. It is my decision. So how do I allow them to love me?

First, I let the gospel break the power of my shame. As long as shame defines me, I will perform for you, but I will not trust you. I will be afraid of what you will do if you discover the "real" me, and so I will keep you at a safe distance, where you can only love my mask. Shame always leaves me unloved—no matter how much love others might have for me.

Second, with the power of my shame broken, I let you love me by revealing my needs to you, needs that my shame always made me hide. God gave us needs so that we can be loved. Because we were designed to be loved, we were created with needs.

In weekend intensives put on by the group Truefaced, participants discuss five God-given needs that are met only through others loving us. The first need is security; love meets this need through commitment. The second need is significance, which love fulfills by affirmation. Our third need, acceptance, is met by unearned love. Next is our need for attention, addressed by servant love that pays attention to the details of our life. Finally, we need protection. I cannot protect myself. The love of others protects me. These needs tell me I desperately need you; it's when I give you permission to meet these needs that I actually *experience* being loved.

Free!
There is only one place safe enough for me to take my carefully crafted shame-hiding mask off and let you see my needs—in the family of God. It's there I have a Father I can trust, and it's there I learn to trust my siblings. And because it is a place where I can trust, it's where I am free, free to be loved.

Summary of Part Three

Everything in a Relationship

My intent in this book has been to allow you to follow my footprints through the good news of gospel freedom—how I discovered freedom in the here and now. And so as I fill in my final spaces on the gospel chart below it becomes the map of my journey to life in gospel freedom.

My adoption into God's family completes my freedom from the controlling power of shame. Being set free from shame is as important as being set free from my guilt—and the blood of Jesus frees me from both. Without living in my adoption, however, I will never know how free I am.

What does adoption set me free for? It frees me to experience all that is mine in my justification and regeneration—in the context of relationship. I have not only been declared righteous; I don't simply walk around with a new nature; in my adoption *God becomes my Father*. Jesus becomes my elder brother. And I have lots of siblings. I am part of a family characterized by love. *Adoption frees me to be loved.*

Adding these freedoms of adoption completes the chart of my journey.

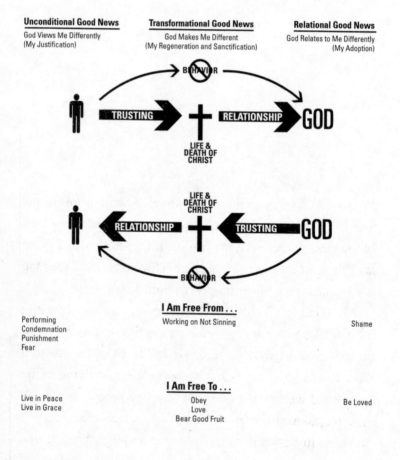

Conclusion

IN THE BEGINNING of this book you met a man who deeply believed in the gospel. Yet as you discovered, that gospel was not transforming my "now." Sure, it gave me lots of guidance on living a good moral life. I didn't use foul language, get drunk, commit adultery, or cheat on my income taxes. It also gave me lots to do to please God—faithful quiet times, Bible study, Scripture memory, witnessing, and so on. But the gospel was not *transforming* me. The gospel was a past and a future good news, but the in-between, the now, was a lot of hard work and effort. You saw my captivity through these pages. And you saw where it led me. I was not free.

Your "in-between" issues may be different from mine.

They might not be leading you to depression and burnout, but unless you allow the gospel to intervene, they will lead you to a place that is not good news. A place of empty gospel promises.

Whatever your issues and whatever your symptoms, the journey to inside-out transformation and to freedom will be the same as mine: you will learn to trust the miracles of the gospel; you will discover that they are *for today!* We may be susceptible to different sins. The enemy may whisper different lies. But the solution for each of us is the same—to live every day in "the glorious freedom of the children of God" (Romans 8:21, NIV).

Notes

INTRODUCTION
1. Tim Keller, *Galatians for You* (Purcellville, VA: Good Book Company, 2013), p. 131.
2. Brennan Manning, *The Relentless Tenderness of Jesus* (Grand Rapids, MI: Revell, 2004), p. 57.
3. Donald Gray, *Jesus: The Way to Freedom* (Winona, MN: Saint Mary's Press, 1979), p. 12.
4. William R. Inge, quoted in *Quotes for the Journey* (Colorado Springs: NavPress, 2000), p. 25.

CHAPTER 1: INTO DARK DEPTHS
1. Macrina Wiederkehr, *A Tree Full of Angels* (San Francisco: Harper Collins), p. 64.
2. Richard Rohr, as quoted in Brennan Manning, *All Is Grace* (Colorado Springs: David C. Cook, 2011), p. 55.
3. Brent Curtis and John Eldredge, *The Sacred Romance* (Nashville: Thomas Nelson, 1997), p. 83.
4. Curtis and Eldredge, *Sacred Romance*, p. 84.
5. Curtis and Eldredge, *Sacred Romance*, p. 84.
6. Curtis and Eldredge, *Sacred Romance*, p. 85.
7. Brennan Manning, *Abba's Child* (Colorado Springs: NavPress, 1994), p. 25.

CHAPTER 2: GLIMPSES OF FREEDOM
1. I memorized Scripture using The Navigators' Topical Memory System (TMS).

CHAPTER 3: MIRACLE ONE: THE UNCONDITIONAL GOOD NEWS

1. Leon Morris, quoted in John Stott, *The Cross of Christ* (Downers Grove, IL: InterVarsity Press, 1986), p. 105.
2. Wayne Grudem, *Systematic Theology* (Grand Rapids, MI: Zondervan, 1994), p. 206.
3. Stott, *The Cross of Christ*, p. 65.
4. In Parts Two and Three we will investigate two additional miracles of the gospel, but this one is foundational to so many aspects of our freedom that we need to carefully unpack it here.
5. Stott, *The Cross of Christ*, p. 173.
6. Brennan Manning, *The Ragamuffin Gospel* (Sisters, OR: Multnomah, 1990), p. 74.
7. G. K. Chesterton, quoted in Brennan Manning, *The Ragamuffin Gospel*, p. 18.
8. Stott, *The Cross of Christ*, p. 148.
9. Athanasius, quoted in J. D. Greer, *Gospel* (Nashville, TN: B&H , 2011), p. 46.
10. Grudem, *Systematic Theology*, p. 724.
11. C. S. Lewis, "The Weight of Glory," in *The Weight of Glory and Other Addresses* (Grand Rapids, MI: Eerdmans, 1965), p. 10.
12. Timothy Keller, *Galatians For You* (Purcellville, VA: Good Book Company, 2013), p. 143.

CHAPTER 4: FREE FROM PERFORMING FOR LOVE AND RELATIONSHIP

1. Milton Vincent, *A Gospel Primer for Christians* (Bemidji, MN: Focus, 2008), p. 5.
2. John Calvin, *Calvin's Commentaries: John* (Albany, OR: Ages Software, 1996).
3. D.A. Carson, *The Gospel According to John* (Grand Rapids, MI: Eerdmans, 1991), p. 520.
4. Lloyd Ogilvie, in Brennan Manning, *The Ragamuffin Gospel* (Sisters, OR: Multnomah, 1990), p. 184.
5. Brennan Manning, *The Relentless Tenderness of Jesus* (Grand Rapids, MI: Revell, 2004), p. 50.
6. Thomas Aquinas, quoted in Peter Kreeft, "Joy," www.peterkreeft .com/topics/joy.htm.
7. Leslie Weatherhead (1893-1976) was an English preacher and theologian. *This is the Victory* (London: Hodder & Stoughton, 1940).
8. Calvin, *Calvin's Commentaries: John*.

NOTES

9. Calvin, *Calvin's Commentaries: John.*
10. Carson, *Gospel According to John*, p. 522.
11. Brennan Manning, *Lion and Lamb* (Grand Rapids, MI: Baker, 1986), p. 19.
12. Paul Tripp, *A Shelter in the Time of Storm: Meditations of God in Trouble* (Wheaton, IL: Crossway, 2009), pp. 33–34.
13. Homer A. Kent, Jr., commenting on Matthew 27:45 in *The Wycliffe Bible Commentary: New Testament*, ed. C. F. Pfeiffer and E. F. Harrison (Chicago, IL: Moody Press, 1962).
14. Brennan Manning, *A Stranger to Self-Hatred* (Denville, NJ: Dimension, 1982), p. 11.
15. Irenaeus, *Against Heresies*, 2.13.3.
16. Manning, *Stranger to Self-Hatred*, p. 12.
17. Calvin, *Calvin's Commentaries: John.*
18. Brennan Manning, *Reflections for Ragamuffins* (San Francisco, CA: HarperOne, 1998), p. 247.

CHAPTER 5: FREE FROM CONDEMNATION

1. Wayne Grudem, *Systematic Theology* (Grand Rapids, MI: Zondervan, 1994), p. 773.
2. He was also punished as an outcome of his condemnation, but condemnation and punishment—the subject of the next chapter—are two different things.
3. Dietrich Bonhoeffer, *Ethics* (New York, NY: Simon & Schuster: 1995), p. 67.
4. Wilbur B. Wallis, commenting on 1 Timothy 1:14-16, in *The Wycliffe Bible Commentary: New Testament*, ed. C. F. Pfeiffer and E. F. Harrison (Chicago, IL: Moody Press, 1962).
5. Duane Liftin, commenting on 1 Timothy 1:16, in *The Bible Knowledge Commentary: An Exposition of the Scriptures*, ed. J. F. Walvoord, R. B. Zuck, and Dallas Theological Seminary (Wheaton, IL: Victor Books, 1985).

CHAPTER 6: FREE FROM PUNISHMENT

1. Leon Morris, *The Cross in the New Testament* (Grand Rapids, MI: Baker, 1965), pp. 190–191.
2. John Stott, *The Cross of Christ* (Downers Grove, IL: InterVarsity Press,1986), p. 124.
3. Samuel Bolton, *The True Bounds of Christian Freedom* (Edinburgh, England: Banner of Truth, 1964), p. 23.
4. Henry Alford, *Alford's Greek Testament: An Exegetical and Critical*

Commentary, vol. 4, part 1 (Grand Rapids, MI: Guardian Press, 1976), p. 241.

5. Bolton, *True Bounds*, p. 25.
6. Gerhard Kittel, *Theological Dictionary of the New Testament*, vol. 4 (Grand Rapids, MI: Eerdmans. 1967), p. 518.
7. Bolton, *True Bounds*, p. 24.
8. Wayne Grudem, *Systematic Theology* (Grand Rapids, MI: Zondervan, 1994), p. 810.
9. Grudem, *Systematic Theology*, p. 810.
10. Bolton, *True Bounds*, p. 46.

CHAPTER 7: FREE FROM FEAR
1. Eugene Peterson, *Christ Plays in Ten Thousand Places* (Grand Rapids, MI: Eerdmans, 2005), pp. 39–40.
2. Peterson, *Christ Plays*, pp. 42–43.
3. Leon Morris, *The Expositor's Bible Commentary*, vol. 12, *Hebrews Through Revelation*, ed. G. W. Barker and F. E. Gaebelein (Grand Rapids, MI: Zondervan, 1981), p. 346.
4. Ann Voskamp, *One Thousand Gifts* (Grand Rapids, MI: Zondervan, 2010), p. 148.
5. Voskamp, *One Thousand Gifts*, p. 161.
6. Brennan Manning, *The Ragamuffin Gospel* (Portland, OR: Multnomah, 2000), p. 218.
7. Philip Yancey, *The Jesus I Never Knew* (Grand Rapids, MI: Zondervan, 1995), p. 38.
8. Steve Brown, *A Scandalous Freedom* (New York, NY: Howard, 2004), p. 246.
9. Brennan Manning, *Prophets and Lovers* (Denville, N.J.: Dimension, 1976), p. 80.
10. Brennan Manning, *The Furious Longing of God* (Colorado Springs: David C. Cook, 2009), p. 82.
11. R. C. Trench, quoted in D. A. Carson, *The Gospel According to John* (Grand Rapids, MI: Eerdmans, 1991), p. 677.
12. Steve Brown, *Three Free Sins, God's Not Mad at You* (New York, NY: Howard, 2012), p. 101.
13. Ralph Wardlaw, quoted in M. R. Vincent, *Word Studies in the New Testament*, vol. 3 (Peabody, MA: Hendrickson, 2009), p. 437.
14. Donald P. Gray, *Jesus: The Way to Freedom* (Winona, MN: Saint Mary's College Press, 1979), p.15, emphasis added.
15. *Luther*, directed by Eric Till (Beverly Hills, CA: MGM Studios, 2003).

NOTES

CHAPTER 8: FREE TO LIVE IN PEACE

1. Bruce M. Metzger, *A Textual Commentary on the Greek New Testament* (Stuttgart, Germany: United Bible Societies, 1975), p. 511.
2. Kenneth Wuest, *Romans in the Greek New Testament* (Grand Rapids, MI: Eerdmans, 1955), p. 77.
3. Bryan Chapell, *The Promises of Grace* (Grand Rapids, MI: Baker, 2001), p. 105.
4. John Campbell Shairp, *Let Me No More My Comfort Draw* (n.p., 1871).
5. Wuest, *Romans in the Greek New Testament*, p. 77.
6. John Stott, *The Cross of Christ* (Downers Grove, IL: InterVarsity Press, 1986), p. 192.
7. Donald Gray, *Jesus: The Way to Freedom* (Winona, MN: Saint Mary's College Press, 1979), p. 38.

CHAPTER 9: FREE TO LIVE IN GRACE

1. Lewis Sperry Chafer, *Grace* (Wheaton, IL: Van Kampen, 1922), p. 81.
2. Kenneth Wuest, *Romans in The Greek New Testament* (Grand Rapids, MI: Eerdmans, 1955), p. 77.
3. William D. Mounce, *Basics of Biblical Greek* (Grand Rapids, MI: Zondervan, 2009), p. 222.
4. Mounce, *Basics of Biblical Greek*, p. 223
5. John R. W. Stott, *The Message of Romans* (Downers Grove, IL: InterVarsity Press, 1994), p. 140.
6. D. E. Hiebert and F. E. Gaebelein, eds., *The Expositor's Bible Commentary*, vol. 11, *Ephesians Through Philemon* (Grand Rapids, MI: Zondervan, 1981), p. 440.
7. John Calvin, *Calvin's Commentaries* (Albany, OR: Ages Software, 1988), Titus 2:12.
8. Gerald G. May, *Addiction and Grace* (San Francisco, CA: HarperCollins, 1988), p. 4.
9. May, *Addiction and Grace*, pp. 4, 16.
10. John Stott, *The Message of Galatians* (Downers Grove, IL: InterVarsity Press, 1968), p. 133.

SUMMARY OF PART ONE

1. Bryan Chapell, *The Promises of Grace* (Grand Rapids, MI: Baker, 2001), p. 93.
2. Chapell, *The Promises of Grace*, p. 93.

CHAPTER 10: MIRACLE TWO: THE TRANSFORMATIONAL GOOD NEWS

1. John Murray, *Redemption: Accomplished and Applied* (Grand Rapids, MI: Eerdmans, 1955), p. 151.
2. Wayne Grudem, *Systematic Theology* (Grand Rapids, MI: Zondervan, 1994), p. 699.
3. Murray, *Redemption*, p. 120.
4. Lewis Sperry Chafer, *Grace* (Wheaton, IL: Van Kampen, 1922), p. 24.
5. Murray, *Redemption*, p. 98.
6. J. D. Greer, *Gospel: Recovering the Power that Made Christianity Revolutionary* (Nashville: B&H, 2011), p. 225.
7. Brennan Manning, *The Furious Longing of God* (Colorado Springs: David C. Cook, 2009), p. 125.
8. Tim Keller, quoted in Greer, *Gospel*, p. 225.
9. Brent Curtis and John Eldredge, *The Sacred Romance* (Nashville, TN: Thomas Nelson, 1997), p. 5.
10. Curtis and Eldredge, *Sacred Romance*, pp. 108-109.
11. Michael John Cusick, *Surfing for God* (Nashville, TN: Thomas Nelson, 2012), p. 102.
12. Ann Voskamp, *One Thousand Gifts* (Grand Rapids, MI: Zondervan, 2010), p. 116

CHAPTER 11: FREE FROM WORKING ON NOT SINNING

1. The truths in this chapter and the next have drastically changed how I pursue spiritual growth—my own and those I help. I want to acknowledge my deep thankfulness and indebtedness to my dear friend Bill Thrall for walking so patiently with me as I slowly shed a paradigm of growth that did not work and was destroying me. The thinking that follows I owe to Bill. And I owe him a changed life.
2. Charles Spurgeon, *The Metropolitan Tabernacle Pulpit*, vol. 31, *Sermon #1823* (London: Banner of Truth, 1971), p. 92.
3. N. T. Wright, *Evil and the Justice of God* (Downers Grove, IL: IVP Books, 2006), p. 89.
4. J. F. Walvoord and R. B. Zuck, *The Bible Knowledge Commentary: An Exposition of the Scriptures* (Wheaton, IL: Victor Books, 1985), Colossians 3:5-6.
5. A. T. Robertson. *Word Pictures in the New Testament* (Nashville: Broadman, 1931), Colossians 3:5.
6. Norman Geisler, commenting on Colossians 3:5, in *The Bible Knowledge*

Commentary, ed. John Walvoord and Roy Zuch (Wheaton, IL: Victor Books, 1983).

CHAPTER 12: FREE TO OBEY

1. Ann Voskamp, *One Thousand Gifts* (Grand Rapids, MI: Zondervan, 2010), pp. 45–46, 59.
2. Wayne Grudem, *Systematic Theology* (Grand Rapids, MI: Zondervan, 1994), p. 724.
3. Craig Keener, *IVP Bible Background Commentary: New Testament* (Downers Grove, IL: InterVarsity Press, 1994).
4. John Calvin, *Calvin's Commentaries: John* (Albany, OR: Ages Software, 1998), John 14:17.

CHAPTER 13: FREE TO LOVE

1. Ernest de Witt Burton, *A Critical and Exegetical Commentary on the Epistle to the Galatians* (Edinburgh: T&T Clark, 1921), p. 279.
2. John Chrysostom, quoted in Joel Elowsky, *Ancient Christian Commentary of John* (Downers Grove, IL: InterVarsity Press, 2007), p. 115.
3. John Calvin, *Commentary of the First Epistle of John* (Logos Bible Software 4), 1 John 3:18-19.
4. Gregory of Nyssa, quoted in Joel Elowsky, *Ancient Christian Commentary of John* (Downers Grove, IL: InterVarsity Press, 2007) p 115.
5. Sermon by Mark Bates, senior pastor, Village Seven Presbyterian Church, Colorado Springs, September 29, 2013.

CHAPTER 14: FREE TO BEAR GOOD FRUIT

1. John Calvin, *Calvin's Commentaries: Romans* (Albany, OR: Ages Software, 1998), Romans 7.

SUMMARY OF PART TWO

1. Sinclair Ferguson, *Children of the Living God* (Carlisle, PA: Banner of Truth, 1989), pp. 41–43.

CHAPTER 15: MIRACLE THREE: THE RELATIONAL GOOD NEWS

1. J. I. Packer, *Knowing God* (Downers Grove, IL: InterVarsity Press, 1973), p. 181.
2. Packer, *Knowing God*, p. 181.
3. John Murray, *Redemption: Accomplished and Applied* (Grand Rapids, MI: Eerdmans, 1955), p. 165.

4. Dan Culver, ed., *Reclaiming Adoption* (Adelphi, MD: Cruciform, 2011), p. 12.

5. Culver, *Reclaiming Adoption*, p. 14.

6. Trevor J. Burke, *Adopted into God's Family* (Downers Grove, IL: InterVarsity Press, 2006), p. 93.

7. Packer, *Knowing God*, p. 181.

8. Sinclair Ferguson, *Children of the Living God* (Edinburgh, UK: Banner of Truth, 1989), pp. 6, 10.

9. Packer, *Knowing God*, p. 190.

10. Colin Brown, ed., *The New International Dictionary of New Testament Theology*, vol. 1 (Grand Rapids, MI: Zondervan, 1975), p. 254.

11. Ferguson, *Children of the Living God*, p. 53.

CHAPTER 16: FREE FROM SHAME

1. Edward T. Welch, *Shame Interrupted* (Greensboro, NC: New Growth, 2012), p. 1.

2. Welch, *Shame Interrupted*, p. 125.

3. Paul Eppinger with Charles Eppinger, *Restless Minds, Quiet Thoughts* (Ashland, OR: White Cloud, 1994), p. 11, emphasis added.

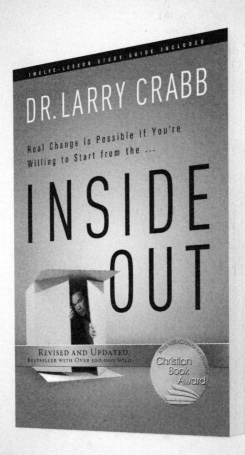

IS AN IMPOSTOR ROBBING YOU OF GOD'S LOVE?

"Honest. Genuine. Creative. God-hungry. These words surface when I think of the writings of Brennan Manning. Read him for yourself—you'll see what I mean!"

Max Lucado, New York Times bestselling author